LINCOLN BIBLE INSTITUTE

W9-BQY-194

WALTER RUSSELL BOWIE

Preaching

ABINGDON PRESS
New York • *Nashville*

PREACHING

Copyright MCMLIV by Pierce & Washabaugh

All rights in this book are reserved.
No part of the book may be used or reproduced in
any manner whatsoever without written permission of
the publishers except brief quotations embodied in
critical articles or reviews. For information address
Abingdon Press, 810 Broadway, Nashville 2, Tennessee.

Library of Congress Catalog Card Number: 54-5508

SET UP, PRINTED, AND BOUND BY THE
PARTHENON PRESS, AT NASHVILLE,
TENNESSEE, UNITED STATES OF AMERICA

251
B78
c.1.

WITH ADMIRATION AND AFFECTION

TO

HENRY SLOANE COFFIN
Who both in the pulpit and out of it
Makes clear the grace that comes from God

11584

Foreword

THIS book deals with one aspect of the work of the man who feels himself called to the ministry of our Lord. But let no one think that this aspect is thought of, or can be held, in isolation. Preaching is part of something that is wider and larger. It is a particular expression of the one purpose which holds all a man's ministry together: that he may try to be a living link between the needs of men and the sufficiency of God. That purpose may be fulfilled in many ways. The minister must lift up the hearts of a congregation in worship that will wake their adoration because he himself in his prayers and devotions has kept close to God. He must be the pastor and counselor who is concerned for all the individuals of his flock. When he baptizes individuals into the family of Christ, and when he administers the Lord's Supper at which that family is gathered together; when he blesses in God's name a man and a woman at their marriage, and when he reads the service for the dead; when he devotes much time and thought to organizing his church for genuinely Christian service—he is making it plain how many-sided the ministry must be. All this is remembered, and all this is the background for the consideration here of how preaching should be conceived. If the emphasis is on preaching, it is on preaching in relation to all the rest. Let that be understood, and then it will be rightly seen that preaching is the making articulate of nothing less than the whole message that comes through a man's relationship to God and to his people.

For such a purpose to be fulfilled, the man who is to be a true preacher of the gospel must learn and keep on learning. The flame of the truth he is to preach has come from God, not from himself; but he himself must take that flame and with dedicated and disciplined skill make it a light for the guidance and help of human souls. As F. W. H. Myers imagined the apostle Paul saying:

> Let no man think that sudden in a minute
> All is accomplished and the work is done;—
> Though with thine earliest dawn thou
>   should'st begin it
> Scarce were it ended in thy setting sun.[1]

I, for one, have had brought home to me this fact that learning is never finished. After more than twoscore years of preaching, I see increasingly how wide and wonderful is the preacher's opportunity, and how one's estimate of what he has already understood is forever being humbled and his perception of what he ought to strive for all the more exalted. In four seminaries—the General Seminary and Union Seminary in New York, the Philadelphia Divinity School, and the Theological Seminary in Virginia, either as a member of the regular faculty or as conducting special but long-continued courses—I have seen young men approach this matter of preaching with the clear and saving simplicity of knowing that they knew nothing. Sometimes as the years go on, men lose that first humility and are in danger of becoming satisfied

[1] *Saint Paul* (London: Macmillan & Co., Ltd., 1908), p. 6. Used by permission of St. Martin's Press, Inc.

8

and complacent. George William Knox, one of the most brilliant theologians of the early 1900's, said once to a group of men going into the ministry: "Gentlemen, remember that your profession is subject to twin vices: laziness and conceit." If a man becomes conceited, he will be lazy too; and so he will cease to grow. But all of us need to remember that though the years have taught us something, there is always the exciting more to which we should move on. Only thus can we be not unprofitable servants, but authentic messengers for the Master of all life.

WALTER RUSSELL BOWIE

Contents

CHAPTER ONE

What Is Preaching?

PREACHING begins where all public speaking begins. Effective public speaking is the effort to communicate to a group of people what one intensely believes and feels, in order to interest, persuade, convince, and move.

"But that is beyond me," many a man may instinctively say—and especially the man who is contemplating the endless succession of sermons he must preach if he is in the ministry. "How can I hope to move a congregation by spoken words of mine?" he asks himself—asks himself as the boy who is questioning whether or not he dares to go into the ministry, or as the man already in it on some day when discouragement has got him down. As flatly as Mark Antony in *Julius Caesar*, and more sincerely, he may say, "I am no orator, as Brutus is," but only "a plain blunt man."

Actually, though, the key to the matter belongs at a different point. It is not the gift of native eloquence that makes a man significant as he speaks to other men, whether in the world at large or in the pulpit. It is the fact that he has got hold of something—or something has got hold of him—so interesting and so important that he can hardly keep still about it. One day he finds himself saying it out, perhaps to a crowd, because that is the instinctive and inevitable thing to do.

There is a man whose simple job it is to be responsible for

13

the door at one of the dormitories of a metropolitan seminary, to take in and sort out the mail and receive packages that may be delivered, to answer the telephone, and at the end of the day to wash the tile floor and leave the entry clean. The last idea he might have of himself would be as a public speaker. But he has a natural mechanical gift through which he has developed in his free time a device that increases the effective energy of the coal burned in a steam engine. He is in the process of securing a patent for it. Ask him about it, and immediately his face brightens, and he will begin to tell about it with animated clearness. Suppose it should be said to him, "A lot of the men would be interested in this. Come on over the next time there is a student meeting and tell them of it." If he thought of that suggestion in terms of "making a speech," he would be struck with consternation and would declare that he could never do it. But if his mind is filled, as it is, with the idea that fascinates him, there simply is not room for hesitation to get in. As long as he is thinking entirely of what he has to tell, he can tell it as directly and un-self-consciously to a group of men sitting before him as he would to one man who stops to ask him a question as he meets him in the hall. Under that impulse he can actually become the public speaker which he might have supposed that he could not conceivably be. It is his consuming interest that has made the difference.

Suppose, says James A. Winans in his book which has these two words for its title, that no one had ever heard of such a thing as "Speech Making." Then:

Here comes a man who has seen a great race, or has been in a battle, or perhaps is excited about his new invention, or on fire with enthusiasm for a cause. He begins to talk with a friend on the

14

street. Others join them, five, ten, twenty, a hundred. Interest grows. He lifts his voice that all may hear; but the crowd wishes to hear and see the speaker better. "Get up on this truck!" they cry; and he mounts the truck and goes on with his story or his plea. A private conversation has become a public speech.

Into that speech, as into all speaking that is to be effective, the essential elements of personal conversation will still be carried. The man will be speaking now to a crowd, but he will need to do so with the same directness and humanness as though he were talking to individuals one by one. He must be sensitive to every sign of changing moods, so that he may not lapse into a self-absorbed soliloquy. Even though it may not look so, what he is engaged in is a dialogue. The audience is speaking too and not less actually if not out loud. People in it are saying to themselves, "That is so," or, "That is not so." At different moments they can be eager or only acquiescent, interested and alertly questioning or gradually growing dulled and bored, attracted or repelled. The spoken word that will be powerful is that which makes the listener acknowledge not only that "this man is saying something exceedingly important to him," but also that "here is something that he is making important to me."

Thus every speech, and likewise every sermon, needs to have the intimacy of man-to-man conversation. It also has larger aspects, but these should always magnify and not obscure the quality of a vital contact between the man who speaks and those who hear. It will widen its range to meet the varied comprehension of the many listeners. It may catch fire from a group response and rise to nobler heights of utterance. But the heart of the matter is the double fact: content and communication. The man must be telling, as we have said, what he intensely believes and feels, and trying with everything

15

that is in him to make others think and feel in that same way.

No one who has lived in the twentieth century can be in doubt as to the possible power of the spoken word. The demoniac voice of Adolf Hitler changed the fate of Germany. He roused the fanatical interest of the German people in the passionate program of the Nazi party, persuaded them of his ability to turn that program into fact, filled them with his own conviction, moved them to gigantic action. Mussolini in equally spectacular fashion had swayed the passions of the Italian people from his balcony in Rome. Winston Churchill, in a better cause, in the dark days after Dunkirk and through the desperate years to follow lifted his countrymen to his own conviction that "we shall never surrender," and taught them so to bear themselves that "if the British empire lives a thousand years, men shall still say this was their finest hour."

Can preaching have such power as that? When the man who has to preach asks himself that question, he may hesitate about the answer. "Ideally, yes," he says, if he remembers the apostle Paul, Chrysostom, Bernard of Clairvaux, Savonarola, Martin Luther, John Knox, John Wesley, Phillips Brooks. and others who could be named from our own day. "But what does that have to do with me?" he wonders. "They were geniuses, and I am no genius." Yet to say that is to miss the greater truth. There is no certainty that all those men were geniuses, if genius means superlative personal gifts with which a man is born. Was Amos, the shepherd of Tekoa, a genius? Was John the Baptist? Was Dwight L. Moody? Certainly they would never have said that "genius" was what moved them. What did move them was the Spirit that came upon them and made their whole selves incandescent in its flame. Any great conviction may do that in a man, but the uniqueness of the preacher is that he can be mastered by the convic-

16

tion that is supreme. He believes that God has something immediate to say to human souls and that God will actually say part of it through him.

Consider the limitless significance of that fact. The preacher is not an unattached and unrelated individual, expatiating upon some amiable but perhaps unimportant ideas of his own. He is a channel of communication from the living God to the living souls who are there before him. As Martin Buber has profoundly set forth in his *I and Thou*, God speaks to us in and through human relationships. He reveals himself to the preacher as that preacher feels himself part of the needs, the hopes, the longing, of all humanity, and as he reaches out in God's name to the men and women whose faces look up to his in order that he may draw them, with their poignant and personal needs, together with himself into the light of a redeeming gospel. And what is that gospel? It is the proclamation that something incomparable has happened and is happening now: that in Jesus Christ—his life, his death, his resurrection—there stand revealed the tragic power of human sin both in history and in our own hearts, and at the same time the love of God which reaches out to save. When the man who goes into the pulpit remembers that, then what he says there—even when his personal gifts are limited—has an exalted significance beyond all ordinary speech. He is there to tell of a mighty fact which can make life different for everyone who hears it.

Anders Nygren, Bishop of Lund, in *The Gospel of God*, by vivid illustration has shown what this can mean. During the Second World War the countries of northern Europe lay under the blight of hostile occupation. Then came the overthrow of the invading power and the message "Denmark is free! Norway is free!" That was the *fact*, but the fact had to

17

be conveyed to all the people—to the underground, to all those who had felt enslavement so long that it was hard to hope—before their life could actually rise up in freedom. "Had that objective fact not taken place, had not a more mighty power come and struck down the oppressor, things would have remained as they had been." But also it was true that "so long as the news of that which had taken place had not reached the individual who lay in prison or who was in hiding, it was as if nothing had happened." Only when both things were realized, "when victory was objectively won and the news of it was spread over the land, only then did the chains fall off, the fear disappear, and men could return to decent human living." [1]

So it is with the preaching of the gospel. It is the proclamation of a decisive event. The power and love of God in Christ have broken the control over men of the evil to which they were in bondage. That power and love, alive and operative, bring the eternal promise: "I came that they may have life, and have it abundantly" (John 10:10). Charles Kingsley, when someone asked him what was the secret that made him the man he was, answered, "I have a Friend." The glory of preaching is to tell men that they do have a Friend and to make their hearts as well as their minds believe it—a Friend who is stronger than wickedness and stronger than worldliness, and who by his immortal power can set them free from every degrading force that holds them down.

Certainly when a man thinks of his preaching thus, he will be both humbled and inspired. He will be humbled because he knows that what he is called to say is beyond his power adequately to express. He will be awed out of any conceit and showmanship. But he will be inspired just because his business

---

[1] Nygren, The Gospel of God, pp. 29, 31.

is so great as to call for everything that is in him—and for what is *not* in him and which therefore he must trust the Holy Spirit to supply. Many may ultimately echo what Albert E. Day wrote in *An Autobiography of Prayer:*

At the beginning, sermon preparation was an agony to me. . . . Until I learned the art of receiving through prayer! Then sermonizing became an act of "listening"—listening to God. . . . If He called me, He had something he wanted to say through me. . . . Therefore, without abating my own diligence in reading and study and meditation, I would look expectantly to Him, to take all my mental and spiritual efforts and illuminate and guide them into the truth He wanted my people to hear, and to add the creative touch which would make of scattered truths and miscellaneous insights a living and convincing unity of ideas. So sermonic labor for God became spirit listening to God. After that the task became a joy. Sermons were still far from what I wanted them to be. . . . They still are! But at least something was given to me—and increasingly through the years.[2]

Thus every commissioned minister can dare trust that God has "something to say through me." How wonderful therefore is his opportunity! He is to try to bring to men and women the ineffable message of what the great apostle called "Christ in you, the hope of glory." He is to interpret to them the meaning of the redeemed life which is the shared inheritance of the Christian fellowship. He is to knock at the doors of human hearts and wills—a courier of God to summon them to the wideness of life and service which is the fulfillment of their real selves.

Nothing less than that is what the man in the pulpit can intensely believe and feel, and to no less an end does he seek to interest, convince, persuade, and move.

[2] (New York: Harper & Bros., 1952), p. 29. Used by permission of the publisher.

SUGGESTIONS FOR SUPPLEMENTARY READING

It has seemed to be of use, from among the almost numberless books that have to do with homiletics, to list here and at the end of each succeeding chapter a few, mostly recent ones, which may be especially helpful for further reading in relation to the aspects of preaching suggested in this book.

Brooks, Phillips. *Lectures on Preaching.* New York: E. P. Dutton & Co., Inc., 1907.

Ferris, Theodore P. *Go Tell the People.* New York: Chas. Scribner's Sons, 1951.

Horne, Charles Silvester. *The Romance of Preaching.* Boston: Pilgrim Press, 1914.

Jordan, G. Ray. *You Can Preach!* New York: Fleming H. Revell Co., 1951.

CHAPTER TWO

The Man in the Pulpit,
The Congregation, and the Message

UP TO A POINT, as we have seen, preaching is like all significant public speaking, natural and direct as spontaneous speaking ought to be. But preaching is also something more. Why that is and how that is grow plain as we ask certain obvious questions. If effective speaking is a man's effort to express to a group of people what he intensely believes and feels, in order to interest, persuade, convince, and move, we still want to know what that belief of his is, and why and in what direction he wants to move those whom he convinces. Political spellbinders may sound so passionate that a crowd is swept off its feet, but it will not be going anywhere. The stronger and more determined man, possessed of fiery eloquence, can carry a nation with him down disastrous ways of his own ambition. The wrong man in the pulpit can win the applause of the unthinking. He can rally people to his egotistic notions and fill them with his fierce prejudice. But what he represents is nothing but the pretense of preaching. The authentic preacher has a purer purpose and a different-centered power. His belief is not in himself, but in Another. In mind and heart he is God's man. Whether his personal gifts are large or small, he commands attention;

21

for in his voice are the accents of an authority that is higher than the voices of this earth. When he speaks, men listen, as they have always listened to those from whom they catch the mightier sense that "thus saith the Lord."

In every preached sermon there are three elements, and these three are included in the sovereign reality that must control them all. These three are the preacher, the people, and what the preacher means to say—or, in equivalent terms, the man in the pulpit, the congregation in the pews, and the substance of the sermon. Each and all of these have their worth only as they are kept in constant reference to God's inspiration, God's compassion for human souls, God's saving truth.

1. Obviously we begin with the preacher himself. There can be no preaching until there is the man to preach. This man is an individual, and he is marked out for his own particular and individual opportunity. No man is to be an imitator of some other man. If he is called to preach at all, he is called to preach out of the direct integrity of his own mind and heart. He is to remember that, though many other men may be interpreters of God and many of them more brilliant and able interpreters than he, no other man can bring exactly that interpretation of life and man and God which he himself can give if with reverent simplicity he looks at truth from the angle of his own personal experience and tries to tell in honest words what he has seen. Those are thrilling words which were put into the mouth of the great maker of violins:

> 'Tis God gives skill,
> But not without men's hands: He could not make
> Antonio Stradivari's violins
> Without Antonio.[1]

[1] George Eliot, "Stradivarius."

God by a miracle might make anything he chose, including the perfect violin—yes. But not even God could make the violin that Antonio Stradivari made without Antonio to make it. So in the message that God desires to be given to his people some note is lost if any man despises the contribution that can be his own; and, on the other hand, from the humblest pulpit in the land can come some special accent and quality of the gospel if the man who preaches there is bravely faithful to what God has revealed to him.

Thus each man is to be himself, but that is not all: he must be his best self. He is not to be the man as merely human forces mold him. He is to be the man made different by his contact with the divine. Henry Sloane Coffin in one of his illuminating books, *Communion Through Preaching*,[2] tells of a great Scottish preacher in an earlier century who kept the congregation waiting for a long time while he tarried in the vesting room. At length some of those who had grown impatient sent the sexton to knock at the door and find out why he did not come. The sexton returned and said that his knock was not answered but that he heard the preacher walking up and down, apparently talking to someone else. This other was not heard to answer, but the preacher kept saying to him, "I cannot go, I will not go, unless you go with me." And the historian adds that when he did come forth and enter the church and climb up into the pulpit, "he was singularly assisted."

In the final chapter of *Go Tell the People*, Theodore P. Ferris has dealt with "Personal Problems of the Preacher," and these are the five he lists: pressure, dryness, doubt, nervousness, and a feeling of ineffectiveness. Any one of these, or all of them, may sometime fall upon a man with a discouragement

[2] Pp. 33, 34.

23

that is almost paralyzing; and he cannot get out from under by any little devices of his own. He must learn what old Brother Lawrence in his wise simplicity called "the practice of the presence of God," so that when he has a sermon to preach or any other compelling thing to do, he may say, as Brother Lawrence said, "Lord, I cannot do this unless thou enablest me"; and when he fears that he may have failed, he will come to God again with words like those which Brother Lawrence used, "I shall never do otherwise if you leave me to myself; 'tis You must hinder my falling and mend what is amiss." [3]

The practice of God's presence—that cannot be a casual matter. It takes time, and it takes quiet; and too many would-be preachers allow themselves to think that they cannot manage these. Or rather, perhaps, it is hardly correct to say that they think so. The trouble is that they do not stop to think about this great necessity at all, but let themselves be carried along half-submerged by the current preoccupations and details which almost drown them. The greatest temptation in the ministry of our time may be that men think themselves so busy that they can seldom or never withdraw into that shrine of quiet where they can be dwelling with God. There is so much they are obsessed to do that they forget what they must be and what they must become. It is quite true that life and the responsibility of a minister under the conditions of our modern world are more complicated and distracting than they used to be. Parochial organization is more demanding. The many forms of community service which call upon a minister for his counsel and for his membership on committees are more imperative. A man may not turn his back upon what

[3] *The Practice of the Presence of God the Best Rule of a Holy Life.* Tr. from the French.

24

may often be these wearying expressions of his ministry in the midst of the kind of world in which he finds himself. But however difficult it may be, and all the more growingly important because it is difficult, he must try to keep the balance between his outward activities and his inner calm. When all is said and done, his supreme business is not to give one more push to one more set of wheels; his business rather is to bring into the complexity and clatter of men's affairs the far look and the steady perspective which will help them see the great ends which alone can give meaning to what they do. Too many men have nothing to preach about on Sunday because they have not kept themselves within that atmosphere of the thought of God which would have preserved their perspective through the week. They have not echoed the Psalmist's words, "Be still, and know that I am God." Instead they have been ejaculating, "Stop, I hear the telephone!" To get away from this nervous compulsion of our overactive age is not an easy thing, and young men particularly at the threshold of their ministry will need to realize that it is not easy. Yet to adopt and to continue steady habits of personal prayer; to keep at the beginning and end, and somewhere too in the midst of the crowded day, a little oasis of solitude and silence where one's thoughts are alone with God; to read the Bible and to think of its meaning not merely as grist for sermons but first of all as food for one's own hungry soul; to worship God oneself, secretly, humbly, and appealingly, and not merely be forever conducting formalities of worship before the people—all this is the vital necessity to which a man must be true in order that he may stand up in the pulpit and tell men something which has truly come from God. If his inspiration fails and he knows that in his thought and in what he tries to say there is only dryness, he may well ponder what Joan of Arc said to

25

the King of France in George Bernard Shaw's *Saint Joan*. Charles, the king, complained to Joan, "Why don't the voices come to me? I am king, not you." And Joan replied: "They do come to you; but you do not hear them. You have not sat in the field in the evening listening for them. When the angelus rings you cross yourself and have done with it; but if you prayed from your heart, and listened to the thrilling of the bells in the air after they stop ringing, you would hear the voices as well as I do." [4]

It is fitting, too, that something should be said about the minister in his everyday relationships with other men if that minister is to be the preacher to whom they will listen with respect. Sometimes there is a strange gulf between a man's occasional piety and his habitual behavior. Some men in the ministry seem to think that, when they are out among the people, they must adopt their standards if they are to be popular. There are ministers who will drink, and gamble, and swear, and suppose that the crowd with whom they are currying favor will thereby consider them to be "good fellows." As a matter of fact, the average man will look at them with a faintly veiled contempt. Of course he has no use for a minister who is sanctimonious or who looks down upon him. If he is going to like that minister, he must feel that they two are men who in friendship and understanding can walk on the same level; but deep in his heart he does not wish this to mean that the minister comes down to his level. He wants the minister to make his own level—the level of a man who walks with God—so attractive that he will try to get up to it himself. He wants that minister in his own sobriety, his cleanness, and his cheerful comradeship to exemplify the kind of standards which

[4] Copyright 1924 by Bernard Shaw. Used by permission of Dodd, Mead & Co.

nearly every man secretly approves and wants somebody to make convincing. When this man goes and sits in the pew on Sunday, he does not want to listen to someone who he knows has truckled to him and to his crowd. He wants to feel that the man who speaks to him is the kind of man who quietly and unostentatiously but unwaveringly has been showing the way ahead toward the kind of life in which every man finds his fullest self-respect.

2. Thus far we have been thinking particularly of the preacher. Let us turn now to a consideration of the people.

A sermon is not an academic performance. The man in the pulpit ought not to be like a boy in school standing up to speak a piece. Yet sometimes that is exactly what he seems to be doing. He has prepared something sitting down in a room by himself on a weekday, surrounded, perhaps, by commentaries and books of various sorts, while he labored to put in some kind of formal shape a notion which he had picked up somewhere as a proper pulpit subject. The fact is that "preaching a sermon" may be a calamitous phrase. It is the phrase, of course, that is habitually used; but it may unconsciously warp a man's ideas from the very start. It bristles with didacticism. It suggests someone standing off at a distance and hurling rounded periods like cannon balls at submissive listeners. It certainly does not suggest something simple, glowing, intimate.

But if the preacher has really brooded imaginatively over his congregation, he will do something more than "preach a sermon" in the stiff and formal meaning of the word. On the days when he is getting the sermon ready, every thought that passes through his mind ought to be warmed by the recollection of the people who on that next Sunday morning may be

27

listening to what he says. It is well that at some time he should go into the church and kneel there in one of the pews and remember those who will be sitting there. Here in one place will be a businessman, burdened and often bewildered by the difficulty of keeping his business from being a failure and at the same time keeping himself a Christian. Here will be a woman bringing in her heart some secret wound of domestic wretchedness. Here will be the young man undecided whether to resist or welcome some hot temptation. Here, seated side by side, will be two who have fallen in love and before whom life seems to be opening into the wonder of a new romance. Here they are, these different personalities with their different joys and sorrows, their opportunities and their needs. What can the message he plans to preach on Sunday be made to mean to them? How can he take what might be a correct but unrelated doctrine and make it throb with the wideness and the wonder, the passion, the pathos, and the pain of human life? If he begins to think of the sermon thus and to search his own mind and heart in the light of his people's needs, then on Sunday his sermon will not be a sort of artificially prepared and beribboned package of ideas which he, the preacher, is handing over at arm's length to the preached-to. Rather it will be the living communication of something so glowing in his mind and heart that the minds and hearts of those to whom he preaches will glow in response. Such a preacher will begin to measure up to the desire expressed by President Howard P. Lowry of Wooster College when he spoke one day in the chapel at Union Seminary in New York. "Someone of you, for all I know," he said, "may some day be my minister. I should want you to be in some sense an expert in theological knowledge, as I should expect expertness from a doctor or lawyer. But the biggest thing I should want from

28

you is not philosophical ideas but a deep consciousness of the meaning of the soul of man in its relationship to God. I should want you to have some interpretation of that fundamental self in every man of which most men are only dimly conscious."

If a man is to preach to people in this fashion, not like an orator haranguing a crowd, but as one man speaking intimately to another, then first of all the preacher must have known his people one by one. All his parochial faithfulness will flow into his preaching to warm it and quicken it with the pulse beat of understanding and affection. Now and then we hear it suggested that the work of the ministry should be so arranged that some men should have nothing to do but preach. "Let these individuals who are gifted in utterance be set free from other duties," someone says, "so that they may spend all their time developing the finest sermons which can be produced." That sounds like a plausible idea, but it is one which would very soon perish if put to the test. Real sermons do not grow out of academic air any more than roses will bloom cut off from their roots. A man may give his people learned doctrines and even bright theological and ethical curiosities for their intellects to play with if his preaching comes out of his own unrelated life; but if he is to feed their souls, he must preach out of an awareness of the everyday living which he has seen and shared with them. In the biography of one of the most winsome preachers of recent times, Bishop David Hummell Greer, it is written concerning his sermon preparation that when his notebooks "failed to start his mind upon a sermon for the coming Sunday, he would leave all his books behind him, put on his hat, and go out; not, as he said, 'for physical exercise, though that perhaps would help, but for human exercise, for the exercise of his heart, his soul, his mind in the midst of human life.' " He would go, continues his biographer, to one

29

or another of the host of his friends; he might go and see an aged woman who had been put out of her home; "he might go and see a devout woman in a cultivated home; he might visit a poor man at his bench; he might go to a house where there were many children and look into their eyes; and the trust and the friendship which he would receive he would bring into his study, and his subject for the coming Sunday would be given him." [5]

This simple and direct friendliness is, of course, the one first basis of human understanding; but it may be supplemented by much else. One of the sources of enlightenment to which no minister of today should allow himself to be blind is psychology. The average minister will not be a learned psychologist, much less a psychiatrist; and he had better not pretend that he is such. But every man can make himself intelligently acquainted with the great suggestions which psychology and psychiatry give concerning the human mind and conduct and character. His preaching will be the surer if he knows how men's ideas and conclusions are actually formed and knows how complex a thing the human personality is, with its impulses and its instincts which go deeper than the level of conscious thought. Those who remember how great throngs of people used to crowd into the Riverside Church to hear the preaching of Harry Emerson Fosdick may not be equally familiar with the fact that he gave many hours each week to individuals who poured out to him their personal problems and distress, which he helped them to understand and deal with. Not only did he exercise a ministry of incalculable blessing for those immediate persons, but what he learned thus of human souls and what goes on within them gave to his preaching to

[5] C. L. Slattery, *David Hummell Greer* (New York: Longman's, Green & Co., 1921), p. 82. Used by permission of the publisher.

the multitudes its almost unparalleled insight and penetration. So he could say, as he did one day, that to him "preaching is personal counseling on a group scale."

A man's knowledge of people and his ability to interpret them to themselves will be fortified too by everything that he may know of history. The story of human life is very long, and the same forces which are at work in men today are those which have been at work through unnumbered generations. The preacher who has read widely and pondered much of history may stand superior, as many men do not, to the gusty passions, the excitements, and the fears which move those who imagine these to be some new dismaying thing which men have never grappled with before. If a man's sermons are made up out of his reading unrelated to contemporary life, they will be, as has already been suggested, external and remote. But if his knowledge of history has been kept close to the heartbeat of his own interest in life, then by all that he has learned of the way in which men have lived and struggled in many centuries will he be the better able to reveal to the immediate men and women there in the pews the struggle which at this instant is going on in and around themselves.

3. Given the preacher and the people, there remains the substance of the sermon. That is a matter which may seem too easy to some and dismayingly much too hard to others.

One man may say to himself, "I like people, and if they like me, they won't be asking for something elaborate. They'll expect me just to talk to them, and that's what I'll do." So he does "just talk," and the result may be summed up in the two words with which a stalwart old bishop characterized the sermon of one of his young clergy, "miscellaneous volubility."

When a man has this casual approach to a sermon, he re-

31

veals his shallowness. He supposes that if he can wangle a few notions from somewhere, they may be a substitute for work. But he is doing dishonor both to his people and to the greatness of the gospel he ought to be proclaiming.

To the people, first. They do not sit in the pews to hear just a talk. It is a serious thing to consider what a congregation is giving as it settles itself to listen to what is spoken from the pulpit. Time is life, and when the twenty minutes or half an hour of the sermon is multiplied by the number of people in a church, there is a significant period of time and life which the preacher will either enrich or waste. A cynical outsider may think of preaching as Anthony Trollope expressed it in *Barchester Towers*: "There is, perhaps, no greater hardship at present inflicted on mankind in civilized and free countries than the necessity of listening to sermons.—Excuse me, my insufficient young lecturer.—To me, it all means nothing, and hours are too precious to waste." But most congregations are wonderfully generous and expectant toward a preacher. They do not demand some pre-eminent utterance, and they are not troubled by a preacher's honest limitations. They will accept with a touching gratefulness any genuine truth he brings to them. But they have a right to expect the best—the thoughtful and disciplined best—of which the man who speaks to them is capable. And if a preacher compels them to say, at length, like Trollope, we refuse "to yawn over your imperfect sentences, your repeated phrases, your false pathos, your drawlings and denouncings, your hemming and hawing," then someone should tell this preacher, as Hamlet told the ranting players, "That's villainous."

Or perhaps the indifferent preacher has another excuse. "Why can't I trust to inspiration?" he likes to ask. "Instead of all this planning and preparation, why not wait for the Holy

Ghost to come down as he did upon the apostles at Pentecost?"

As to that it is true that the Holy Ghost did come like tongues of fire upon the heads of the apostles, but it is also true that there was something inside their heads for the fire to kindle. They had their memories of their Master, the truths they had learned from him, the convictions they were eager to find a new way to express. That is always the way with the Holy Spirit. It will descend as flame, but if it is to become a burning and a shining light, it must have fuel through which it can spread its fire; and that fuel is the fit and ordered thought which a man has tried to bring together in his mind. If the Holy Spirit ceases to be manifest, the reason may be wrapped up in one short and simple word. When Martin Niemöller came to the United States after he had been released from a concentration camp, he said that the long imprisonment had seemed at first to leave his power of mental co-ordination so weakened that for a time he could not bring himself to make any systematic plan for what he was called upon to preach. He had to trust, he said, to the moving of the Spirit; and the Spirit will come to the man who knows that he is at the end of his own strength. Then Niemöller paused and looked at the seminary students to whom he was speaking. "All that is true," he said, "but don't presume upon it. Do not think that the Holy Spirit will do what you ought to do. In one of the synods of the Evangelical Church in Germany a young minister testified that he never prepared his sermons, but trusted the Spirit to put the right words into his mouth. When the turn came for an older man to speak, he said, 'We heard our young brother say that he did not need to prepare his sermons because the Holy Ghost would speak to him and tell him what to say. As for me, the Holy Ghost never spoke to me in the pulpit. Yes, I remember, he did speak to me once. When I was going down the pulpit steps after a poor sort of sermon, the Holy Ghost spoke to me. He said only three words, and what he said was, "Heinrich, you're lazy." ' "

As the man who is lazy about his preaching does dishonor to the people who have a right to expect his best, so also he does dishonor to the majesty of the truth he is supposed to try to interpret. He acts as though the great message deserved no more than cheap methods. Contrast the attitude of the dedicated interpreter in another field. On March 25, 1952, Arturo Toscanini had his eighty-fifth birthday. That week he had been rehearsing his orchestra by nine in the morning and in afternoon sessions that lasted from two-thirty to seven. The day after his birthday he remarked that it had been fifty years since he first conducted Beethoven's *Ninth Symphony*, "and I am still far from getting it." "A prodigious statement, calling for another Toscanini to grasp its full significance," wrote the music critic who reported what Toscanini had said.[6] A prodigious statement, yes; but one the parallel suggestion of which ought to be grasped by any preacher who has some conscience for what he is called to do. For if the great conductor felt that after a lifetime he still had more to learn about interpreting the music of Beethoven, so that "there can be no slips," how can any man dare to bring only an extemporaneous and complacent jauntiness to the interpretation of the Word of God?

If it is a fact that some men treat preaching as though it could be easy, there are those on the other hand who fall into the opposite mistake of being appalled because it seems so hard. What should be preached, and what might be preached if a man felt capable, seems so vast and awful. In the abasement of his spirit a man of today may be like Moses, standing

⁶ Robert Bagar, New York World Telegram and Sun, Mar. 29, 1952.

before his vision of the burning bush, "afraid to look upon God." Like Moses he may cry when the voice from the flame bade him go and carry God's message to the people, "Who am I, that I should go? . . . They will not believe me, nor hearken unto my voice."

But the reassurance that can come is a double one. It is first from God, in words like those to Moses, "I will be with you." If a man truly is ready to give all that he has, both of obedience and of ability, to God, he is not left alone. He can move on to accomplishments which at first might have seemed impossible, for always the mightier help will be at hand. At the time of his sudden death in 1949 one of the most influential preachers in America was Peter Marshall. Growing up as a poor boy in Scotland, he worked at nights in a foundry near Glasgow; and when he was twenty-three, he came to the United States as an immigrant. Although he had had no college education, the opportunity opened for him to go to a seminary; and he made his way into the ministry. Through the last twelve years of his short life, as he stood in the pulpit of the New York Avenue Presbyterian Church in Washington, great crowds of people flocked to hear him and found their hungry spirits richly fed. "Always he felt inadequate," wrote his wife, "for the tasks to which God called him, but because he knew God had called him, he also knew he would get the help he needed." [7]

Reassurance comes also through the men and women for whom a sermon is prepared and to whom it will be preached. One cause of the dismay a minister may feel as he faces the task of constructing sermons is that he may see his task in

[7] *Mr. Jones, Meet the Master* (New York: Fleming H. Revell Co., 1949), p. 10. Used by permission of the publisher.

terms of vast abstractions. Theological truth seems so un-bounded and so intricate. How can he ever make it plain to people? But the answer is that he does not have to make it all plain at once, but only to tell as truly and worthily as he can some part of it that is growing clear to him. And, further-more, it is not a one-way matter. A man does not have to un-derstand the height and depth and width of the revelation of God by merely pondering this for himself and trying to tell others what he supposedly has mastered. Rather he learns the wonder of this best as this revelation comes back to him from the lives in which he has seen it actually expressed. Many a minister might grow very fainthearted in his faith if he had only himself to depend on for his assurance. But week by week he can be fortified in the gospel he is preaching as he sees that gospel attested in men and women who would never get up in the pulpit and put into words what they think and feel. When he preaches about God, he can remember those who are putting their shoulders beneath their loads with a strength which is inexplicable except that it comes from God. When he preaches of Christ, he can remember this man or this woman in whose daily self-forgetfulness he has seen the mean-ing of a Christlike life. When he speaks of the life eternal, he can remember those in whom there has been revealed a quality of life that God will not let die. Again and again and in in-numerable ways his gospel passing through his appreciation of his people will come back to him enriched.

So the fashioning of a sermon will never be easy in the sense of a casual something that involves no effort. But if it is not and ought not to be easy, it can be all the more exhilarating. For it is like the long, courageous breaking of a new trail up a mountain, along which afterward a man may guide his friends to where they may look up with him together to the Alpine summits of the glory of God.

SUGGESTIONS FOR SUPPLEMENTARY READING

Henrichsen, Margaret K. *Seven Steeples*. Boston: Houghton Mifflin Co., 1953.

Jowett, J. H. *The Preacher: His Life and Work*. New York: Harper & Bros., 1930.

Marshall, Catherine. *A Man Called Peter*. New York: McGraw-Hill Book Co., 1951.

Neill, Stephen C. *Fulfill Thy Ministry*. New York: Harper & Bros., 1952.

Spann, J. Richard, ed. *The Ministry*. New York and Nashville: Abingdon Press, 1949.

CHAPTER THREE

Three Aspects of the Preacher's Opportunity

WE HAVE THOUGHT of the factors which combine in the preaching of a sermon. What shall be said of the qualities which should appear, if not in every sermon, or at any rate not with equal emphasis, yet somewhere in a man's whole preaching? In the full scope of that preaching from month to month and year to year various sides of the prism of truth must contribute their light and color to his message if in richness of value it is to be complete.

1. First, the *mediatorial*. The man in the pulpit must be a meeting point between the needs of human souls and the rich promise of the grace of God.

Sometimes this function of the preacher is forgotten because it is submerged in something else. There are those who tend to think of the minister as mediator only at those moments when he is to them specifically the priest. They want above all to see him standing, as the priests of Israel did, not in a pulpit but at the altar, lifting the prayers and offerings of the people up to God. And also in churches that do not dwell in thought or terminology upon a priestly conception of the ministry, even there it may happen that people begin to wonder about the value of preaching and to think that perhaps all they need is to be led in worship. It was in this century that a clergyman of a great metropolitan church created a wide sensation by declaring that there ought to be a "moratorium on preaching." And the mood out of which such an idea may grow is reflected in these sentences from a magazine article by Bruce Barton:

> Faith and courage and peace are not of the mind; they belong to the spirit. By the music, by choir, . . . by silent prayer, or by meditation alone in a beautiful chapel, they are conducted from the Great Something to the something within. They are not conducted by argument. Except "ye become as little children." . . . Little children do not argue. They wonder and feel.

As to the ineffable significance of worship, in which not only the mind but the whole being is made aware of God, he is right. Everywhere in Christendom that is being increasingly understood. Witness the sensitive perception expressed in the booklet prepared in 1936 by the Federal Council of Churches on Seven Principles of Public Worship. But "faith and courage and peace are not of the mind; they belong to the spirit"—that is not a true antithesis. Faith and courage and peace may be mediated through the whole being of the man who stands up to preach and in that preaching uses the utmost that God has given him of mind and heart and will to inspire all these in the men and women who listen to the message that he brings.

We do wrong to the manifold glory of God if we set up an attempted contrast between worship and the word. Every sermon ought to be in some great sense a sacrament. For what is a sacrament? It is an "outward and visible sign of an inward and spiritual grace." Yes, and it may be an outward and audible sign too. There is the sacrament of the Holy Communion in which the bread and the wine become the symbols of the presence of Christ himself and of living fellowship with him. He ordained that sacrament. But did he ordain any less a sacrament when "he ordained twelve, that they should be with him, and that he might send them forth to preach," and when at the last he said, "Go ye therefore, and teach all nations," and in connection with *that* gave to his disciples the promise, "Lo, I am with you alway even unto the end of the world"? If bread and wine may be the channels of his communication, shall not a living soul be the channel of his communication too? Of course it is possible for a man in the pulpit to defeat his opportunity. If he is shallow and strident, he will destroy rather than fulfill the service of worship in which his sermon has part. But by and large if a man's life is rooted in worship, and if he comes into his pulpit overshadowed by the consciousness that he is meant to be a messenger of God, then faith and courage and peace will be mediated not only in worship apart from him. In the long run, for thoughtful people grappling with the real world there will be need of his interpretation to make them know that the consciousness of the divine which has come to them when they are worshiping can stay with them when they go out of the sanctuary into the noise of the workaday world. The realization of this is nothing novel, nor should it seem to be confined to any particular part of the Church of Christ. It was a friar of early fifteenth-century England who wrote:

It is more profitable to hear God's Word in preaching, than to hear any Mass. . . . For by preaching folk be stirred to contrition, and to forsake sin and the fiend, and to love God and goodness; and be illumined to know their God, and virtues from vices, truth from falsehood, and to forsake errors and heresies. By the Mass they be not so; but if they come to Mass in sin they go away in sin, and shrews they come and shrews they wend. And also the virtue of the Mass standeth principally in the true belief of the Mass, and especially of Christ that is there sacred in the Host. But that may men learn by preaching of God's Word.[1]

If the man in the pulpit is to be at the same time in this high sense the mediator between the needs of his people and the living reality of God, he must look out upon the people with a sensitive understanding. He must ask himself why they have come to church. It is true that many of them might not be able to give an explicit answer. There will be those who have come through habit or convention. There will be those who have come with some real inner urge, but without the ability to explain to themselves what that urge is. But all the while they want something which he must try to give. They want the living bread which the preacher must supply.

There before him will be the empty souls. In those pews will be sitting men and women for whom life may have seemed to drop into dust and ashes. Some terrible disappointment or defeat has turned their experience into a desolation. Or perhaps the thing that has happened to them is not sudden and catastrophic but only a drying up of the source of life's inspiration. Little by little the springs of their ideals and their faith have silted up. The dust of the world's business has covered their spirits so that all the face of things seems colorless and arid, and no great thoughts and purposes are flowering in them any more. Wherever they look, life seems so empty of fragrance or of beauty that they almost wonder whether it is worth while to exist.

There is the need, too, of the guilty souls. In every congre-

---

[1] Quoted in Charles Smyth, *The Art of Preaching:* A Practical Survey of Preaching in the Church of England, 747-1939 (New York: The Macmillan Co., 1940), p. 16.

gation there are those who have just faced, or tremble to think that they will face tomorrow, the results of the disclosure of their own wrongdoing, their unfaithfulness, or their incompetence, too long unrepented of and uncorrected. Here is the man who secretly has been a thief and a defaulter, who finds himself caught in the closing net of his derelictions and wonders whether there is any strength in himself and any mercy in his world by which he can get free. Here is a man who has played fast and loose with some human relationship and now faces the humiliation of having others know of his weakness and of his sin. Here is the parent who looks back on long years of stupid blundering with his child and sees that child, now grown, turn against him with all the accumulated resentment which has been suppressed in the years during which it had to endure a father's or a mother's irritability and impatience. Here is someone who has had a great opportunity for achievement and has thrown it away through a lazy unconcern which took advantages for granted and did nothing to develop the increasing power by which alone they could be deserved. All these people and many others like them may be staggering under the secret burden of their guilt. To their world they may present a hard face. They may pretend that they are still successful and satisfied, but the weight of the inward load they carry grows heavier and heavier. Like that immortal figure whom John Bunyan drew in *Pilgrim's Progress*, they walk everywhere with a weight upon their back; and they are wondering desperately how long it will be before they go down under it—or whether there is any such thing as the grace of God which can loose it and lift it off.

And then there is the need of bewildered souls. Many of those who came to maturity in and after the First World War thought of themselves as the "lost generation." The old land-

42

marks seemed to them to have been destroyed. Their elders did not appear to know, and therefore they could not discover, what the dependable directions of life's efforts and ambitions might be. And though the phrase "a lost generation" is an exaggeration as applied to any one single group, nevertheless the suggestion of the words has continuing truth. There are numberless people who in greater or less degree are lost. They are groping for a sense of meaning in life that they do not find. In their search for satisfaction they seem to go around in a circle. They get a temporary excitement, but no lasting inspiration. They see plenty of lights that glare in the streets, but they wonder whether there are any principles which are steady like the stars. They may walk on the "great white way," but it does not seem to lead anywhere except into a whirlpool. Are there any straight vistas, they wonder, leading out into spaciousness and expansion for their souls? If there are such, they have not found them; and wistfully thus beneath even their most pathetic bravado of assurance, they carry the deep fearfulness of those who feel that they are lost.

But there may be a need even deeper than that of the so-called "lost generation." Those who could be described by that word knew that there was something they were lost *from*. Somewhere back in their tradition were great faiths which they remembered at least had once seemed sure, and so perhaps might some day be recovered. But after the long, drab disillusionment that followed the First World War's glittering promise of the earth made new, and after a second conflict of more bitter consequence than the first, there has come a generation that feels not so much lost as beaten. The "lost generation" were rebelling against an accepted code of behavior, to which, when the rebellion was over, they might return. But a newer generation feels naked in mind and ultimately in soul—without standards, without security, without even acquiescence. The president of a midwestern college, telling of the breakdown of a student honor system which for a long time had operated successfully there, wrote:

In the past few years the quality of student conduct has suffered seriously. Behind individual violations of hitherto accepted standards lies a set of attitudes, a "climate" directly opposed to what we say we believe in. These attitudes include, among other things, the ideas that: freedom is inherited, not earned; an individual should have complete freedom; any experience is educational; what I do is my personal affair and nobody else's business. The net result is that the moral base of the college is nearly nonexistent. This phenomenon is widespread. The causes are multiple and complex. Among them are: the present national and international tensions, the impact of the draft and the general level of morale in a society which feels itself in transition but does not see to what end.[2]

Other societies also have been in transition, but they have had more generally accepted compasses to steer by. In the middle of the 1800's the religious faith of numberless people was shaken by the new pronouncements of the physical scientists which seemed to destroy the authority of the Bible. It was an "awful moment when the soul began . . . to feel the nothingness of many of the traditionary opinions which have been received with implicit confidence, and in that horrible insecurity begins also to doubt whether there be anything to believe at all." In such a time Frederick W. Robertson fortified his faith "by holding fast to those things which are certain still—the grand, simple landmarks of morality. . . . If there be no God

[2] Edward L. Nestingen, *Church Review*, May, 1953 (Church Society for College Work, Washington Cathedral, Mount St. Alban, Wash., D. C.), with quotations from an article by Clellon Holmes in *New York Times*, Nov. 16, 1952. Used by permission of the author.

and no future state, yet even then it is better to be generous than selfish, better to be chaste than licentious, better to be true than false, better to be brave than to be a coward." [3]

The preacher of today may believe as Robertson did, but in preaching to the bewildered and beaten in his generation he cannot assume that to them the "grand, simple landmarks of morality" will seem "certain still." He must speak to a profounder need. He must go down deep to lay again for many people the foundations of a faith in God's eternal righteousness on which they can build their moral strength. He must show God's truth in human history and the reality of God as a saving power for present human lives. That will be a supreme task for any preacher, challenging and difficult, but full of inspiration for the utmost he possesses of sympathy, intellect, and faith.

Yet in the manifoldness of life it is a blessed fact that not all the needs a preacher faces are the somber ones.

There are the needs also of joy and of thanksgiving. There are men and women to whom some great unfolding of life has come. These two young married people have just experienced the wonder past all speech of the first baby come into their home. This father and mother are rejoicing because a boy has finished his school with honor and is starting out, clean and clear-eyed and confident, into his first college days this fall. Or to this man has come the promotion in his business, or the honor in his profession, which without any conceit he knows to have been the fruit of a long honesty of purpose and devotion to hard work. Or here is this woman to whom there has just been revealed in some sudden and heartwarming way the results in human gratitude of a service which she has

---

[3] Stopford A. Brooke, *Life and Letters of Frederick W. Robertson* (New York: Harper & Bros., 1865), p. 86.

long been rendering. To all these there has come great enrichment, but in that very enrichment there is need. They want the one further and higher element which will crown that which they have gained. They want to feel the blessing of God upon it. They want to feel that their causes for thanksgiving are like a great ladder reaching up to heaven on which they climb to the assurance that life itself is good and that God is over all.

Of course it is possible for the man who stands in the preacher's place to forget all this. He may be merely uttering unrelated ideas of his own, like an ecclesiastical phonograph rotating through his half hour until the sharp needle of his preoccupation has traveled around the disk. He may be speaking words as in a vacuum, words that he has put together in his study out of all relation to actual flesh and blood. But this man is not a preacher. He is only an ecclesiastical dummy masquerading in the preacher's place. The real preacher will have felt the compulsion of his people. He will have felt it in imaginative sympathy as he got his sermon ready. He will feel it again like the drawing of the tides when he stands up to preach. He will be remembering all the needs he knows and all the needs he does not know, but nevertheless is sure are there. And this compulsion will draw his heart in desire and his words in eagerness. It will be woe to him if he cannot say something, the utmost something that mind and heart can compass, to the manifold and pulsing need which confronts him there.

Thus the man in the pulpit can be at that same moment the mediator who makes the people aware of their spiritual hunger and lifts that hunger up to where it is fed from the fullness of God. This he can be and this he can do if before all else and above all else he has first endeavored to enter himself into a

46

hushed awareness of the light and life, the pardon and peace, which come from God. He will know then that his supreme business is to convey a feeling which has first moved him as by a vibration from the infinite and can be transmitted to the people who look at him and listen to what he says. The reason so many preachers seem shallow and inconsequential is because they do not convey this feeling which is deeper than words; and the secret of the moving power which some preachers have, and which all in some measure at least might have, lies in the fact that through them the unmistakable majesty of God is somehow conveyed. People in the pews hunger for this more than for anything else, even though they may not be able to give it a name. They want to be lifted up into a greater atmosphere than that which they ordinarily breathe. They want to feel that life which often seems so petty and constricted does really open out into vistas which are eternal. Above the dust of common things they want to get a glimpse of the snow-clad mountains. Beyond their cramped perspectives they want to feel the ineffable horizons. Beyond the shores of their islanded affairs they want to hear the calling of the sea. All this the preacher ought to bring them, and he will do it only by the grace of those reflections which his own spiritual eyes have seen and by those echoes which his ears have heard. In technical aspects some particular sermon or many sermons may be a failure, but they are not a failure if through them somehow there has been conveyed to people a sense of awe and wonder, a brooding consciousness of another world, and that strange lift which comes to the humblest human soul when it is made aware that even the little things of the common day are caught up into some grand music of eternity.

2. The second quality that ideally should be in preaching is

47

hard to put into a single word. It has to do with a man's objective and his outreach. What people is he trying to persuade as he preaches the gospel, and what does he want to have happen through such persuasion? His preaching is to be *pastoral, but more than pastoral.* Perhaps the one word which comes nearest to expressing the quality in mind is *appealing*—an appeal to a wide enough circle and with practical result.

In the ordination service in the *Book of Common Prayer* those about to be ordained are charged "to be Messengers, Watchmen, and Stewards of the Lord; to teach, and to premonish, to feed and provide for the Lord's family." Thus is prefigured the intimate ministry, by sermons and by every other way, to the congregation for which the minister is immediately responsible. But a wider responsibility is added. Those to be ordained are charged also "to seek for Christ's sheep that are dispersed abroad, and for his children who are in the midst of this naughty world." For the preacher this means that his preaching must be conceived in terms not only of those who are expected to be in church, but also of the outsiders who are not there but might be moved to come.

There is always a risk that preaching directed continually to the already converted may little by little grow obvious and conventional, and lose its eagerness and urgency. A congregation all amiable and generally sympathetic may be heart-warming, but not challenging. A man may thank God that he is helping his friends and yet be fearful that his preaching may go soft because he does not seem to be confronting the sharp doubts, the aggressive sins, and the flat repudiation of his gospel which he knows would meet him in plenty of places outside his church. How can he come to grips with that sort of resistance, or, in other words, how can he have something so

48

real to say to the "man in the street" that this man will come off the street to hear what he has to say?

The first answer is that he must try to know that man outside the church in every simple human contact that comes his way. He must like him for what he is, while always deep within him is the desire that this man may wake up to see the bigger and better person that the grace of God can make him be. When this emotion is really in the minister's heart, it will get into his preaching. He will be wishing that this man who thinks he has no use for God were there in church, and that longing will put into his sermon the accents which would speak to that man if he did come.

Then, as a matter of fact, one day he does come. It may be by accidental impulse. It may be in cool curiosity. It may be instead because some fierce emergency pushes him into a church in a blind desperation that does not know anywhere else to go. But there he is. The preacher may not know it. He cannot consciously preach to that particular man. But if in the whole hope and purpose of his preaching he has had some passionate desire to bring to such a man God's saving gospel, he will be bringing it now. Dean Charles R. Brown has told of an occasion when he was preaching a sermon on the mercy of God. In the church that night was a young man hesitating between attempted flight or suicide because he had stolen $2,700 from his employers and the theft was about to be found out. Something that he sensed in the spirit of the preacher made him go to Dean Brown after the service and pour out his story —which led to a visit by them both to the employers, the man's confession, an agreement by them to keep him, until through years of work and poverty he paid the money back and in the process recovered his integrity and re-established his life. "Suppose," said Dean Brown, "that I had been trifling with some

49

fringe of the truth that night! Suppose that owing to a lack of preparation or to a lack of genuine feeling I had been unable to make the quality of mercy, human and divine, shine as a thing resplendent in the dark sky which overarched that troubled, guilty soul! I should have been smitten to the heart with shame." [4]

Some such man may be in any congregation, and the quality of preaching which can win one such man is the preaching of which more and more of the "dispersed sheep" will hear and to which silently but surely they may be drawn.

Yet thus far we have been thinking only of preaching to those who have somehow been got into the church. But that is not enough, and to act as though it were enough is to make it possible that a man's ministry will become conventional and complacent and soft. When any man is on fire with a message, he goes to where the people are and does not merely wait comfortably for them to come to him. Remember Jesus, preaching on the hillsides and on the lake shore where the fishing boats came in. So John Wesley and George Whitefield carried the gospel out upon the village greens and into the open fields of eighteenth-century England. So the itinerant preachers, particularly the Methodists and the Baptists, followed the advancing American frontier and took the challenge of Christian faith and life into raw settlements that otherwise might have been godless and degraded. The physical frontier in most countries is almost gone, but not the spiritual frontier. On the other side of that frontier there are great areas of human life that should be won: multitudes of men and women who never come to church, who have no sure convictions or commitments, God's children who know nothing of their spiritual heritage. They will not be reached by routine

[4] *The Art of Preaching* (New York: The Macmillan Co., 1922), pp. 14-15.

sermons at eleven o'clock on Sunday mornings. And the grievous fact is that vast numbers of preachers are not even thinking of how they might reach them. Suppose there were tens of thousands of Communist spokesmen supported by congregations and free to speak wherever and whenever they chose. Would they be as shut-in and satisfied as most preachers are?

In short, we need a rebirth of eagerness and effort in evangelism—and this does not mean a desperate recourse to some professional evangelist to come to a town and accomplish in a week or two what its own ministers neglect. All honor to the men who do dedicate their whole lives to evangelistic preaching, among whom have been preachers of great power, like Dwight L. Moody, and through whom indubitable conversions have come to pass. But evangelistic machinery organized and brought in from outside may fall short in two ways: at its poorest it may be crude in thought and sensational in method, and even at its best it may be transient in effect. Like a sudden storm with thunder and lightning and a flood of rain, it may startle and overawe, and it may seem also abundantly to water the earth; but much of what it brings runs off before it can be absorbed, while what most souls need is stimulus more measured and more constant. That is why the ultimate evangelistic work belongs to all the ministers of Christ and not to the few. No man is fully faithful to his commission unless the urge to evangelistic effort is in his heart. As to methods there can be no stereotype. Imagination must be flexible according to place and conditions and times. A man may hold a series of services in his church, deliberately and devotedly planned for those who have had no use for religion, and get the organized cooperation of his laymen to invite and to bring acquaintances of theirs who belong in that outsider group. He may hold those services instead in a theater or some other nonchurch place.

He may preach at noonday from an outdoor pulpit, if there is one, by the side of his church, or where knots of men gather together in a public park or by a factory. He can talk to little groups of people brought together in somebody's home, and there or anywhere else what he says to a whole gathering can have its best fruit as he makes opportunity for individuals who have been stirred by what he said to come to him alone. In such evangelistic outreach, simple and straight and true, he will not be playing with any petty themes. He will be believing that in almost every human soul there is a spiritual hunger, no matter how much it may be hidden; and he will be seeking to minister to that hunger as he speaks of the hollowness that may come to human lives when they have no inspiration, of all men's need of an uplifting purpose, of Christ's kingdom as a cause to serve, of our own inadequacy and the saving grace of God.

When the preacher of the gospel does have this evangelistic outreach toward human souls, and when his message draws them, what should be the result?

Certainly a true result is not merely the increase of a congregation. Neither is it only the solution of personal problems or the bringing of individuals into a fold where they may be safe—but satisfied and selfish. Here the figure of sheep must give way to another figure that goes beyond it. Samuel McChord Crothers, that preacher and essayist so whimsical and yet so wise, has written in one of his essays of a theological seminary to which was left an endowment with the surprising provision that it should be used to establish a chair of applied military science. With misgivings the trustees created the chair and invited to it a retired colonel, who then proceeded to justify his appointment abundantly by jolting the seminary students out of complacent and conventional ideas. Dr. Crothers writes:

> I confess that I was prejudiced against the new chair, for I am naturally opposed to fads of every description. . . . But when I met the colonel, my fears vanished. He had the fine simplicity of mind that is characteristic of the best men of his profession. . . . Moreover, he was evidently a spiritually-minded and free-minded man. . . . He wondered sometimes what would become of the military qualities he so loved and admired when the war drum throbbed no longer and the battle-flags were furled. It was then that the idea of the world as a spiritual battlefield came to him. Here was a conflict of forces, a good fight to be fought. He looked about for some organization fitted to make a stand against the evils of the world. He realized the significance of the term The Church Militant. That was enough for the colonel. All the ardor of youth was rekindled. He saw at once the irrepressible conflict between those who were banded together in behalf of a spiritual ideal and the forces of sensuality and selfishness. "Here is something," he said, "that can't be arbitrated. It must be fought out. The Church Militant has, I believe, the right of it, but the question is, is it strong enough to win out? Has it mobilized all its forces, and is it prepared to assume the strategical offensive?" [5]

Thus the appeal in preaching must be directed toward some virile result. When Wilfred Grenfell, afterward by his great work in Labrador to become world-famous, was a young medical student in London, he heard Dwight L. Moody preach; and then and there he determined that he would dedicate his life to whatever and wherever it would count for most. Some years later he met Moody and told him of the time he had heard him and of how he had been deeply moved. Moody's response was characteristic. "What have you been doing since?" he asked.

[5] *Among Friends* (Boston: Houghton Mifflin Co., 1910), pp. 195-97. Used by permission of the publisher.

And what have the people "been doing since" who are preached to in the average church? What, for instance, of the man who has been genuinely moved to try to express a new Christian allegiance in his life? What is the answer to him if he asks, "What can I do?" Is it that he be an usher and walk up and down the aisle at the Sunday morning service? Is it that he be an officer of a men's club which has an occasional parish supper and listens to a speaker? Or this woman—what shall she do? Belong to a sewing circle or take care of the vestments of the choir? Any one of these may actually be a dedication, and it is possible for genuine Christian purpose to be expressed through any one of them. But they are not enough. By themselves they do not attract the bad people, and neither do they kindle the imagination of those who, paradoxically, are outside the church because in some ways they are so good. For many men and women who are face to face with the wrongs and evils of their world and acutely want to right them—social workers, visiting nurses who cover the slums, conscientious public officials—the church may too seldom seem to be the power for directed righteousness with which they would want to ally themselves.

3. Therefore preaching at its fullest is not only mediatorial and not only pastoral in the personal sense. Its appeal must have to do also with the moral and spiritual responsibilities people ought to feel, and the best do feel, as members of their communities. The interpretation of God's message must be extended *there*. So in true preaching there needs to be this further quality: it must be *prophetic*.

Many men in simplicity and modesty may shrink from associating that adjective with themselves. Prophetic: that is what the towering figures were, such as Isaiah or Jeremiah.

Yes, but except in degree they were what other men can be. They were the men who because they dwelt with God had profound insight into the conditions of their times and therefore with foresight could proclaim what moral cause and consequence would be.

Beside the great cathedral which stands at the heart of London there is a marker at the spot where from 1116 to 1613 was St. Paul's Cross, the outdoor pulpit "whereat amid such scenes of good and evil as make up human affairs the conscience of Church and Nation through five centuries found public utterance." In modern pulpits also a conscience like that can find expression. Honest and dedicated men can give prophetic interpretation for their own generation. The prophet may not be popular, at any rate not at first. But thoughtful people in the churches, wanting to know what their religion fully means, will be grateful for a preacher who stands up above the crowd and the crowd's confusion to perceive those forces which are driving the whole of life toward evil or toward good, and then will tell them unflinchingly what he has seen.

Obviously there are dangers here. The preacher must not become what a satirical commentator once called the ministers whom he had observed, "men of a gently complaining spirit." Neither must he become a fanatic obsessed by some particular cause which draws him in only one direction like a moth drawn by a blinding light. And above all he must not be a conceited and cocksure declaimer of shallow judgments which he likes to utter because he thinks they will make a sensation. But with these provisos the truth remains that if the pulpit is to be powerful today it must have in it men who can be spokesmen for God in relation to the actual world men live in and the civilization by which their souls are shaped.

This kind of preaching cannot begin with confident advice

about particular problems in business, commerce, industry, or international affairs. It begins—in the preacher's own thought and in his constant emphasis—with the attempt to build behind every immediate question those backgrounds of eternal truth by which all the struggling values of our time are to be measured and corrected. The prophet first of all will be helping his people remember the everlasting reality of God, the moral accountability of man, the sacredness of personality, and the seriousness of life.

But though prophetic preaching does not begin with particular problems, it does go on to these. It can be as direct and devastating as Elijah's indictment of Ahab at the gate of Naboth's vineyard; as specific and unmistakable as the condemnation of social sins in the first chapter of Isaiah, the central chapters of Hosea, and the sixth chapter of Micah; and as terrible as Jeremiah's prediction of the downfall of Judah and Jerusalem before the Babylonians. It grapples with sins like these by the same compulsion which Amos felt when he looked at the iniquities in Israel and said, "I was no prophet, neither was I a prophet's son; but ... the Lord took me ..., and the Lord said unto me, Go, prophesy unto my people. ... Now therefore hear thou the word of the Lord." In the intensity of his moral earnestness Amos saw the civilization around him as a wall along which the hand of God had dropped a plumb line and revealed that wall to be so out of plumb that at any moment it might fall. The whole book of his prophecy particularizes that danger of a social structure in which many imagined that they were safe and prosperous but which was leaning now to its destruction. He dealt not in general terms but in awful plainness with the greed of the rich, the luxuriousness of the prosperous, indifference to human misery, and the kind of injustice that went on as people who had power exploited those who had not. And above all he pointed out how the ecclesiasticism within which smug men tried to warm their consciousness was only a pretense of loyalty to the God whom their daily lives denied. "I hate, I despise your feast days," he cried in the name of the Lord; "take thou away from me the noise of thy songs; . . . But let judgment run down as waters, and righteousness as a mighty stream."

There are times when the preacher who is not afraid to try to be God's spokesman must be as specific as that. He must deal with particular evils in his community, even though they involve the clear truth which those who are there in front of him need to hear and not the recital of somebody else's sins which they might like to hear. He must help his people gain the moral honesty and the moral courage to look beneath the smooth surface of things and see the actual facts with which their conscience is called upon to deal. Particularly in a day when there is so much propaganda always at the disposal of rival interests to confuse and mislead the average well-meaning man, there is supreme need for the contribution which the Christian pulpit can make to the real issues involved in economic, industrial, political, and international conflicts. The preacher must try with all his might to preserve that purity of spirit which will lift him up above the charge of partisanship, but he must not leave his message in ineffective generalities. When he has a chance to speak to men who represent organized labor, not only must he make clear his sympathy with those great aspirations for justice to the worker and for a legitimate share in controlling the conditions of their work by which they may be moved; but he must be bold enough to point out the dangers of dishonest or stupid leadership, of racketeering violence, and of soldiering on the job by which their cause may be corrupted. If he is preaching to more privileged people, among whom are bankers and lawyers and investors in business, his duty is not to please their prejudice by denouncing the violence of labor, but rather to help them see the kind of concealed and gilded but none the less deadly violence which entrenched privilege may be practicing every day through its economic dictatorship and under the protection of the law. Wherever passions arise, it is the business of the prophet to meet them with a cleansing understanding. The Christian pulpit cannot stand silent in the face of anti-Semitism, of injustice to the Negro or to any other weaker group, or of the lies of demagogues who invent their vicious slogans to mislead and to corrupt. Always the prophet can stand as the defender against forces that left alone would lead to moral and spiritual apostasy.

When we have spoken that word "prophet," we may have thought instinctively of the Old Testament; but the Christian preacher is to be a prophet whose perception of the will of God is lighted too by that wider illumination which comes from Christ. The kingdom of God, as Jesus said, is like leaven. It goes on spreading until every fiber of that with which it is associated must feel its quickening power. It is like the mustard seed which, however small it seems at the beginning, springs up into impressive growth. So the thought of Jesus, the judgments of Jesus, and the estimates of Jesus, once they have been let loose in human society, have no end. They go on confronting our accepted evils one after another. They go on forcing us to recognize that such and such an institution or practice or belief, no matter how profitable it may be, is unchristian and, because it is unchristian, must somehow be corrected. The spirit of Jesus follows men into their business and makes them ask disturbing questions there. It goes abroad into the world of relationships between employer and employee, and forces men of sensitive conscience to choose at last on the basis not of what is easiest or of what is most immediately rewarding, but of what in the light of Christian principles will be right. It reaches out into international affairs and rebukes blind nationalism in the name of the oneness of human destiny which is the irresistible will of God. Once these ideals have challenged men, there is no getting "back to normalcy"; and it is these ideals which the man in the pulpit who has in himself some of the prophetic spirit must present.

When a man does try thus to stand as truly as he can in the great succession of those who have been the prophets of the truth of God, he will have much need for courage. He will have need also for common sense. Whether men originally like what he says or not, in the long run they will listen to him if they know that he is honest and that back of what he says are sober thought and solid knowledge.

A very wise and experienced preacher once gave to a younger man the following advice in relation to the preaching which touches disputed issues of community life.

In the first place, he said, do not preach upon such matters as these too often. Nobody is charged with important prophecy that requires public attention every week. A man must not run the risk of seeming to be either a sensationalist or a fanatic, or of confining his preaching to one strident emphasis. Most of his preaching should be of that quiet and simple and personal kind which poor human beings with their own intimate problems to be met are mostly needing. When now and then he does speak as a man under the prophet's compulsion on a matter that has to do with sensitive economic, industrial, or social issues, he will have a greater power if men know that he thus speaks only because he is moved by some irresistible call.

59

In the second place, be sure of the facts. Many a sermon has collapsed and many a preacher has been discredited because, being moved by some sudden impulse, he launched into a rhetorical utterance based on supposed information which he had not checked or verified. When a man mistakes or misinterprets facts and draws an exaggerated picture, he rouses against himself both anger and disgust. The first obligation of the preacher is to say only that which he knows and which, if he is challenged, he can drive home with proof up to the hilt.

In the third place, said the wise old counselor, never make a frontal but always a flank attack. Do not deliberately and needlessly rouse your parishioners to inevitably provoked resistance. Let the truth come upon them in a way which does not give their prejudices a chance to take up arms. It is foolish, for example, to begin a sermon by saying some such thing as this: "I want to preach to you today about the evils of child labor," or "about race prejudice," or "about the duty of supporting the United Nations," thereby rousing the irritation of the man in the pew, who says, "I do not want to hear about child labor, or about race prejudice, or about the United Nations, and what has any of that to do with the preaching of the gospel which I did come to hear?" Let the preacher rather begin by leading his listeners to remember what Jesus said about the preciousness of children, or his parable of the good Samaritan in which the alien was the man who proved himself most worthy in God's sight, or the picture in Revelation of the Holy City into which the glory and honor of all the nations shall be brought. Then when he has won the instinctive sympathy of his listeners and they are wide open to suggestion, he can invite them to consider in what way Christians are obliged to feel about the question which he now unveils, if they are to be true to the spirit of Christ. Thus to men and women who if assailed head-on would stiffen into resistance his approach is instead through the unbarred gates of those indisputable Christian values by the recognition of which his particular message may go home.

When men of this type stand in the pulpit, then the words which Charles Sylvester Horne wrote in his *Romance of Preaching* can come true:

> Show me the man who, in the midst of a community however secularized in manners, can compel it to think with him, can kindle its enthusiasms, revive its faith, cleanse its passions, purify its ambitions, and give steadfastness to its will, and I will show you the real master of society.

SUGGESTIONS FOR SUPPLEMENTARY READING

Garvie, A. E. *The Christian Preacher*. New York: Chas. Scribner's Sons.

Macgregor, W. M. *The Making of a Preacher*. Philadelphia: Westminster Press, 1946.

Niebuhr, Reinhold, ed. *This Ministry*. New York: Chas. Scribner's Sons, 1945.

Underhill, Evelyn. *Concerning the Inner Life*. New York: E. P. Dutton & Co., 1950.

CHAPTER FOUR

Resources for Sermons

GRANTED THAT all that has been thought of thus far is true," a man who is to preach may say, "if I am to prepare a sermon, how shall I begin?" The answer is that he should begin long before he *has* to begin.

Fénelon, Archbishop of Cambrai in France of the late seventeenth and early eighteenth centuries, wrote in his *Dialogues on Eloquence* what preachers, together with all other public speakers, need to remember. He was speaking of those who may seem talented, but have no depth of knowledge. "Their minds seem empty. You see that they have been put to no end of trouble to find the wherewithal to piece out their speeches." And then Fénelon continued:

Immediate preparations, however laborious they may be, are necessarily very incomplete, and the capable man demonstrates this as often as the weakling. You must spend many years in getting abundant resources. After this sort of general preparation, immediate preparations cost little. But if you have only applied yourself to the preparation of particular subjects, you are reduced to paying off in the currency of aphorisms and antitheses; you treat only the commonplaces; you utter nothing but incoherencies; you sew up rags not made for each other; you do not show the real principles of things; you are restricted to superficial and often false arguments; you are incapable of showing the full extent of truth, because all general truths have necessary interconnections, and it is obligatory to know almost all of them in order to handle adequately a particular one.

And still more pungently he refers to the preacher who

thumbs his concordance . . . some sermon books he has bought, and various collections he has made of purple patches wrested from their context and hit upon by good luck. . . . In a case like his, one cannot say anything strongly, one is certain of nothing; everything has a borrowed and patchwork look.[1]

The meaning of all that is plain, and it is crucially important. Real sermons, which will feed people's minds and hearts, cannot be produced on the spur of the moment any more than ripe grain can be gathered from empty ground. There must have been preparation of the earth, sowing of the seed, patient cultivation, and then a justified trust in the long, silent processes of vital growth before the harvest can be reaped.

There is a rich word in the Bible which might well be more in our modern consciousness, and that word is *meditate*. To meditate, says the dictionary, is "to keep the mind in a state of contemplation; to dwell in thought." To *dwell:* mark that. In other words, not to have to run distractedly after some stray idea, but to stand still long enough in welcoming contemplation for thoughts to come to us of themselves. "Isaac went out to meditate in the field at the eventide," says the book of Genesis; and the first psalm tells of the man whose "delight is in the law of the Lord; and in his law doth he meditate day and night." In our twentieth-century world meditation is not easy, but it is all the more essential; and a man does not have to be a philosopher to learn to meditate. What he needs is to cultivate gradually the habit of reflection:

[1] Tr. Wilbur Samuel Howell (Princeton, N. J.: Princeton University Press, 1951), pp. 84-87. Used by permission of the publisher.

reflection upon his own experience, the scene around him and the people he meets, the events of everyday life and the significance in these which the heedless may not see.

"Stop, look, and listen" is the sign one may see at a railroad crossing. There it is a sign of caution. It warns that one should not go blundering into danger. But the same words may well be set up with another meaning before the mind's eye of the man who is to preach, as he goes about in God's world. Instead of a warning it is an invitation—an invitation to stop, look, and listen not for what may hurt him, but for all the beneficent wonder that he can encounter at every turn. If he is not alert, this will not enter into his ken. But for eyes and ears that are open there will be in fields and trees, in hills and rivers, in sky and stars, a presence that disturbs him with the joy of elevated thoughts; in city streets and all the places where people work a continual lesson in what human motives and desires are; and in the ordinary life of men and women and little children, going out and coming home, a revelation of the mingled dignity and pathos of existence for which he needs an understanding heart.

An echo from a line of William Wordsworth's will be recognized in that last sentence, and from Wordsworth has come one of the significant influences affecting human thought. Plenty of poets before him had written greatly on great themes, but he could stand before what had been ignored as commonplace and interpret the greatness of meaning hidden there. He "saw things that other people do not see, and he saw with quite unique clearness and frequency things which they see at most rarely and dimly. This is his originality." [2] And that is the sort of originality which the man who is to preach must

[2] H. W. Garrod, *Wordsworth: Lectures and Essays* (Oxford: Clarendon Press, 1923), p. 95.

try to cultivate. It is freshness of approach to the world we live in. It is keeping the eyes open, the interest keen, and the spirit of wonder everywhere awake. That was the way of Jesus. He was aware of God, and he saw the heavenly truths revealed not only in what to us might have been the conventional places—not only in the synagogue, not only in the times of prayer—but wherever he might be. When he saw a sower scattering seed and watched where the seed fell—on a trodden path, on rocky soil, among the brambles, or on good ground— he thought of men's hearts and of how differently the seed of the Word of God may find, or not find, its rootage there. The merchant always searching for the perfect pearl suggested to him what the search for the kingdom of God should be. A woman kneading leaven into meal was a symbol to him of how God's spirit can permeate the whole of life. The lost sheep and the shepherd, the headstrong boy leaving home, the men who sent their casual excuses to the host who was expecting them to dinner—here again in familiar facts he saw the infinite parallels, the love of God and the folly and faithlessness of which his children can be guilty. Wheat and tares growing together in the field; laborers waiting to be hired; a man giving commissions to his servants; bridesmaids so careless that they missed the wedding; a man beaten on a road, two men straight from the Temple who would not help him and the unexpected man who did—these were the sort of suggestions that struck fire in the thought of Jesus. So when the moment came for him to talk to the disciples, or to the crowds that flocked around him, about God and about their own hearts in relation to God, he did not have to start with some abstract beginning. His parables, vivid and unforgettable, shaped themselves out of what he was observing and reflecting upon every

65

day. Is there any doubt as to what this says to the man who would be a preacher of the gospel now—to the man whose ability to prepare a sermon and to preach it gladly must depend upon what his mind has been storing up long before? It says to him, Look; look at the manifold wonder of God's world; look at life; look at people, and try with reverent understanding to look deep into them; look for the meaning of God that shines through familiar facts. Reflect and meditate, and let the fruit of that meditation be stored up in your mind and heart for the time when it will be called for.

It is important to stress this truth that the man who is to think creatively and bring to others a message that will be vital, as every preacher ought in some measure to do, should begin thus by cultivating the faculty of fresh observation. He must not be caught in the ruts of the secondhand and the obvious, which are so easy for the indolent to accept. When S. S. Mc-Clure came as an immigrant from Ireland to New York City in the 1870's, New York seemed to him then—as he wrote later in his autobiography[3]—to be so immense and overwhelming that imagination could hardly conceive of anything more. Surely, he thought, it was finished; nothing was left to be done. As a matter of fact, it was then a city of three- and four-story buildings, with elevated trains drawn by little steam engines, its cobblestone streets lighted by gas lamps. Instead of being finished, the city was at the beginning of incredible transformation. Limitless opportunities were waiting for those who had eyes to see. And because the young Irish newcomer, at first appalled by his own sense of being in a world that was huge and complete and without any opening for him, got over this frustration and started out courageously on his own,

[3] New York: Frederick A. Stokes Co., 1914.

he went on to become one of the influential publishers and molders of opinion of his time. So the never-finished city and the never-exhausted opportunities in it are a parable of what is true in every realm of life and service. The future beckons to the man who has fresh faith and thought to bring. That is true for the pulpit, and belief that it is so is not a matter of any personal conceit. It is the humble recognition, which yet dares to be bravely honest, that God's truth invites every man to open his eyes to its limitless significance. He may see some aspect of it which has not been seen and interpreted in exactly that same way before. This is the reason why every man who is to preach should observe and reflect and meditate in his own way. If he has had the faithful diligence to do that, then when he has to write a sermon, there will be living springs in his thought from which he may draw.

Nor should observation be only a matter of physical sight. It is a matter also of wider and deeper perception. "Study occasions," wrote John A. Broadus in that fine old book *On the Preparation and Delivery of Sermons,* "seeking . . . the reality of things. Study the general condition of the congregation; reflect upon all special occurrences of religious interest, and upon any secular interest that may furnish illustration." And he went on to say, "Study the age in which we live," and, "Study yourself." A man must look deeply into his own soul and see what experience is writing there if his preaching is to have its maximum reality and moving power. It was said of John Brown of Haddington after his wife's death:

From that time dates an entire, though always deepening, alteration in his manner of preaching. He changed his entire system and fashion: from being elegant, rhetorical and ambitious, he became concentrated, urgent, moving (being himself moved),

67

keen, searching, unswerving. The truth of the words of God had shone out upon him with an immediateness and infinity of meaning which made them, though the same words he had looked upon from childhood, other and greater and deeper words.[4]

Of course, however, there is more to remember. A man should begin with his own thinking, but he is not to stop there. He is to enrich his mind with the wisdom which can come to him from the great thinkers of many generations. In other words, he must read. It is true that if the sermon on Sunday is to be the sort of welcome bread which the congregation will reach out for, it must be made from what has grown fresh and immediate from the field of his own life and thought; but what can be harvested there may be a thin growth unless the ground is fertilized. It is when a man has gathered to himself the utmost he can gain of stimulus and inspiration from great books that he can give most richly also from himself.

In the three-volume *Life and Letters of Phillips Brooks*, by Alexander V. G. Allen, one of the most impressive facts is the revelation of Phillips Brooks's omnivorous reading. It is very rare to find in one of his sermons any direct quotation. He never used extracts from other men's thought as ribbons tied for adornment upon his own theme. But what he did was to pass the raw material of immensely rich and varied reading through his own mind until it became like innumerable golden threads which he then wove into the spontaneous pattern of his own glorious utterance. Back of his preaching and imbued in it are the myriad colors of which no man can be the master unless truth has come to him through the prism of many great minds.

In his *Lectures on Preaching* there is a vivid and reveal-

[4] John Brown, Jr., *Horae Subsecivae* (Edinburgh: Edmonton & Douglas, 1866), p. 12.

ing paragraph which shows in his own words what the long-range result of reading can be:

Constant quotations in sermons are, I think, a sign of . . . crudeness. They show an undigested knowledge. They lose the power of personality. They daub the wall with untempered mortar. Here is the need of broad and generous culture. Learn to study for the sake of truth, learn to think for the profit and the joy of thinking. Then your sermon shall be like the leaping of a fountain and not like the pumping of a pump.[5]

And he also writes:

The preacher's life must be a life of large accumulation. He must not be always trying to make sermons, but always seeking truth, and out of the truth which he has won the sermons will make themselves. I can remember how, before I began to preach, every book I read seemed to spring into a sermon. It seemed as if one could read nothing without sitting down instantly and turning it into a discourse. But as I began and went on preaching, the sermons that came of special books became less and less satisfactory and more and more rare. Some truth which one has long known, stirred to peculiar activity by something that has happened or by contact with some other mind, makes the best sermon; as the best dinner comes not from a hurried raid upon the caterer's, but from the resources of a constantly well-furnished house.[6]

If a man's reading is to be one of "large accumulation," he will need to read the big books—big, that is to say, not necessarily in the number of their pages but in the significance and weight of the matter they contain. A temptation to which many men yield is to fritter away their time with ephemeral magazines or upon equally ephemeral books of the type which are easily read but equally easily forgotten, because there is

[5] Pp. 159-60. Used by permission of E. P. Dutton & Co., Inc.
[6] *Ibid.*, p. 159.

nothing in them to enlist the serious powers of the mind. No better thing can happen to a man than to belong to some group of ministers or to a group of men drawn from various professions who make it their deliberate purpose to match their intellectual sinews against stiff reading. Some pastors, preachers, and theological professors whose ministry was in New York City in the second quarter of this century owe more than they can ever fully acknowledge to a little organization which has been in existence for thirty years and still continues, with a membership of fourteen men. It meets once a month for seven months from October to April, and each spring a list of books is chosen which will be read in the following season, books which are the most important and commanding that the membership can think of in such fields as theology, philosophy, history, biography, poetry, and science. Out of the fourteen men seven are successively hosts at dinner in a season and the other seven are the essayists. In the next year the order is reversed, and the men who were the hosts the year before are the essayists, and the former essayists are the hosts. The significant fact about the whole plan is that each book is to be read not only by the one man who is to review it but by every single member of the whole group, so that in the discussion of the book the informed and thoughtful ideas of every man shall be brought forward. Many men in the ministry nowadays may find themselves in places where there is, or where they can organize, such a group; and if they do, they can find it one of the happiest and most rewarding ventures which any minister can carry out.

Suppose, however, that a man does thus set himself a program of worth-while reading which he wants to carry through, how shall he achieve it? That is a question which cannot be invariably answered, but the nearest, perhaps, one can come to answering it is to say that the time exists if a man has sense enough to seize it. The idea, of course, is that a man should so budget his days that he will have definite hours at certain periods of the week when no ordinary interruptions can reach him and when he can devote himself to the solid and serious reading which he ought to do. But almost equally important is the cultivation of the faculty of using the little fragments of time that so many men unthinkingly waste. Arnold Bennett wrote once an unforgettable essay on *How to Live on Twenty-Four Hours a Day*. His point was that the main problem of life is not how to live on such and such a number of dollars, though certainly this may be urgent enough. The more vital problem is how to live on that exactly measured capital of time in which all men in the course of a year share equally. Out of that capital of 8,760 hours or 525,600 minutes which belongs to every man in the span of a year, a staggering amount may run to waste. Here are the minutes wasted when a man is riding on a railroad train with no worth-while book brought with him and with nothing to do but to "kill time." Here are the minutes wasted on a subway train or bus while the eyes roam aimlessly over the advertising signs. Here are the minutes wasted in a doctor's or a dentist's waiting room, or in some place where one has come for an appointment at which the other person is late. And here are the other odd minutes in nearly every day when a man is idle because he has nothing in his mind to do. Of course it is not to be suggested that one should be a kind of wound-up automaton clicking into action at every moment without any time for relaxation or for the simple friendliness in which people meet and talk together with no ponderous aim to learn something they did not know before. It is not meant that a man should make a kind of

71

fanaticism of being found perpetually with a book. But what *is* meant is that he should cultivate this kind of companionship for the many incidental opportunities which every day may offer.

Yet of course this fragmentary reading will be of signal value—and indeed is likely to be carried out at all—only if it is part of something larger. The man who is to preach must dedicate to his reading not only broken bits of time, but whole blocks of it; and to do this he must have a steady and determined purpose. It is a dreary fact that many men in the ministry do not have this purpose or have lost it if they once had it. Martin Luther wrote indignantly: "Rich folks' children . . . are complacent, arrogant, and conceited, and think they need to learn nothing because they have enough to live on anyway. . . . The poor fear God; therefore he gives them good heads that they may study, become educated and intelligent." He was speaking primarily about material riches, but he might have said the same thing concerning the riches of the mind. There are those who are not only "rich folks' children" but rich themselves in the intellectual privileges they have had, men who have gone to a college and a seminary, and then stop studying because they "think they need to learn nothing because they have enough to live on anyway." There are great ranges of study which they ought to pursue: in the Bible, in theology, in church history, in the record of the words and works of those who have been the interpreters of Christianity all down the years. But many men will not buckle down to that kind of study, and there is no one to compel them. They have a room that they call "my study," but the name and the reality have no connection. They may become like the college student of whom William James once wrote, who would walk up and down in his room, poke the fire, pick up lint off the floor, turn over the pages of the newspaper, waste time any way whatever, rather than apply himself to the one thing he was supposed to do, namely, to learn Jevons' *Lessons in Logic*, which he hated. And though the man in the ministry may not be said to hate the studies he avoids, not even his Hebrew and his Greek, yet he can neglect them as completely as though he did. Why dig deep foundations for his sermons, he may ask himself, when he can "get by" and "put something over" without that? But the result will appear on Sundays. As John Henry Jowett in *The Preacher: His Life and Work* trenchantly observed, "If the study is a lounge, the pulpit will be an impertinence." [7]

But how different the fact can be! The work of the ministry is crowded with many obligations, and ought to be; but the minister has as much time as any other man in a serious profession, and it is a shame to him if he is not as diligent in his own field of knowledge as the physician, the lawyer, the social worker, the scientist, must try to be in theirs. If he deliberately determines to set apart periods in the week which except for unavoidable emergencies will be devoted to nothing but study, he can do it. When his people know what he is aiming at, they will respect his time and will respect him.

Of course he cannot read everything that might be desirable ideally, but it is the quality not only the quantity of reading that counts. He can pursue consistently for a given number of weeks, or for a whole year, some subject which came alive for him in the seminary but will dry up in forgetfulness if he does not help it grow. He can keep up with the most stimulating contemporary books through some such prompting as that of an appropriate book club. Or he can discipline his mind to match the intellectual challenge of the books that

[7] P. 114. Used by permission of Harper & Bros.

have permanent authority by following the list of those which have been named by superlative scholars, such as may be found in the bulletin carrying the recommendations of the heads of departments put forth from time to time by Union Seminary in New York.

Is this a task to which a man must drive himself? On the contrary it is an opportunity so rich in privilege that it ought to wake a wondering and eager thankfulness. The minister who devotes some systematic part of his days to solid and studious reading is doing what every man might covet the chance to do for his own personal enrichment—yet cannot, because the demands of his particular work do not permit it. For such a man steady reading may seem a remote ambition, to be gained only as he gets loose from his main responsibility. But for the minister there is the fact, both challenging and humbling, that work with his books is part of what his congregation directly wants him to do. And if he is diligent and devoted, his reading—even in the hours when he most feels its personal privilege—will not be self-indulgent. In a true sense it can be vicarious. He is reading and thinking with imagined faces around him. Here are the men and women who may not themselves have the opportunity that is given him. They are tied to tasks in the home, the office, the farm, the factory. They cannot spend much time with books. But they have given him a responsibility on their behalf. He is to explore anew great fields of human thought. He is to follow again the visions and aspirations of poets and prophets who have enlarged the dimensions of our human life. He is to listen to those who have been the age-long interpreters of the revelation of God. "This association with the greatest minds of the world . . . is on the intellectual side what we mean by the

74

'communion of saints.' " [8] And from such communion a man can bring to his people, in his pastoral ministry and in his sermons, the food of great thoughts for hungry minds, the fire of inspiration for waiting souls.

All this will be more surely true in proportion as the minister in his study measures up to the standard which the Second Epistle of Peter sets for all Christians—as one who, "giving all diligence," adds to faith virtue, and to virtue knowledge, and to knowledge patience. The life-giving truths which people will be grateful for cannot be appropriated and they cannot be passed on in hasty snatches. The ideas that will enrich a man and give substance to his preaching are not those he gets from some hasty foray on behalf of a sermon that right now must be got ready. They come instead from long wondering, from the patient pursuit of the light that at first is only a distant gleam, from a pilgrimage of the mind that does not depend upon quick rewards. D. Elton Trueblood wrote:

The reading that we ought to be doing in our studies is, for the most part, reading that is not undertaken with immediate sermonic or homiletic needs in mind, just as the best farming is done by men who are constantly building the soil and not merely fertilizing for the immediate crop. If a man is always reading important books such as major biographies, essays, literary studies, science, philosophy, and theology, he can hardly fail to have a significant message. In such reading we run into exciting ideas in the most unexpected places.[9]

But even if a man has learned to read faithfully, one more question must be answered. How is he to remember what he

[8] George A. Gordon, *My Education and Religion* (Boston: Houghton Mifflin Co., 1925), p. 160.

[9] J. Richard Spann, ed., *The Ministry*, p. 176.

has read, so that it may be available when he wants it? When he has supposed he had some fine idea captive, how is he to avoid having to acknowledge—in the words of the prophet to King Ahab (I Ki. 20:40) about *his* captive—that "as thy servant was busy here and there, he was gone."

It is dismayingly true that what we take from books, when we go to look for it, may be gone. The problem is to give it such sure welcome and protection that it will stay with us.

The methods which men have used differ. The important thing is for a man to have a method that is congenial to him and will work. Grand old Alexander Whyte of Scotland

used to complain that he had the worst memory in Edinburgh, and to tell his student-friends, "No one knows the labour that my memory has cost me!" The moral which he drew, for others as well as himself, was "Always read with your pencil in your hand." His children gradually discovered that, while ordinary presents had little attraction for him . . . he had an insatiable appetite for notebooks. . . . A small notebook was always in his pocket to capture and preserve ideas which came at unexpected times.[10]

Henry Sloane Coffin, one of the twentieth-century preachers most notable for the wideness of reading by which his sermons have been enriched, had the custom of carrying with him small cards like those in a library file catalogue. On each of these he would jot down an idea as it came to him or some arresting quotation, under a heading that had to do with some particular aspect of truth or life; and these cards would be inserted into his constantly lengthening file. And if one looked at the books on his study shelves, one would see on the flyleaves within the back covers memoranda which indi-

[10] G. F. Barbour, *The Life of Alexander Whyte, D.D.* (New York: George H. Doran Co., 1925), p. 289.

cated and summarized the features in the book to which he might wish swiftly to turn again.

This chapter therefore ends upon the note of its first emphasis. The time to begin a sermon is long before it has to begin. It should grow out of thoughts and convictions which may have been planted years ago. Left to themselves, the little ideas, like tiny seeds, will blow away with the wind; and the one way to hold them and make them fruitful is to write them down and watch over them until they take root and grow.

SUGGESTIONS FOR SUPPLEMENTARY READING

Allen, A. V. G. *Life and Letters of Phillips Brooks.* New York: E. P. Dutton & Co., 1901. Vol. I, chs. 5-7.

Blackwood, A. W. *The Preparation of Sermons.* New York and Nashville: Abingdon Press, 1948.

Coffin, Henry Sloane. *What to Preach.* New York: Harper & Bros., 1930.

Oman, John Wood. *Concerning the Ministry.* New York: Harper & Bros., 1940.

Roberts, Richard. *The Preacher as a Man of Letters.* New York: Abingdon Press, 1931.

CHAPTER FIVE

On Knowing the Bible

THE SUPREME AREA for a preacher's thinking and for his preaching should be the Bible. That ought to be obvious, but in fact and in practice it is not obvious.

Today many of the young men preparing for the ministry are startlingly ignorant of the Bible. For the most part they were not familiar with it in their boyhood. Some of them have a smattering acquaintance with a few stories remembered from Sunday school, and some have not even that. The beautiful old custom of family prayers, with the accompanying readings from the Bible, has had no place in the homes where they grew up. The Bible was not in their curriculum at college. The seminary to which they come when some inner moving turns them toward the ministry may too often assume—as could be assumed in earlier times—that they do know the Bible and that the foundation of that knowledge is there and can be built upon. But it is not there. The result is that these young preachers-to-be, beginning to study subjects derived from the Bible, take at second hand theological and historical and pastoral-counseling formulations which depend upon a foundation they do not have. Consequently their preaching, when they start on that, is shaky and un-

78

certain. They are like men laying bricks in a wall up in the air, with nothing solid underneath them.

Furthermore it is true that too many men more advanced in their ministry are also neglectful of the Bible. They may sometime have been decently familiar with it, but they have not been mastered by a sense of its immense and everlasting message. To interpret it to the modern age seems to them a more profound and difficult matter than they want to devote themselves to undertake. So they turn to more catchy and casual subjects: to current events, to some bright notion picked up from a magazine, or to amateur psychology. Thus it results that the sermon announcements on many church bulletin boards too seldom suggest the worship and service of God, and too often are tinkling little invitations to some prescription as to how everyone by his own smartness can become a success.

But preaching that is to have the nobility which ought to belong to it must be a "channel, not a source." [1] That is to say, it must draw from something deeper and vaster than the preacher's personal ideas. By themselves they would be only a shallow pool. His thought and his utterance must be the outflowing of a mightier source, and that source is the revelation of the eternal message of God for human life as it is contained in the profundities of the Bible.

The true preacher will turn—as we shall see—to the Bible for his dependable sermon subjects and particular texts. But first he should turn to it in order that he may gain from its majestic scope the perspective on life which he needs and which his congregation needs to learn from him. Our modern generations have little sense of history or of any meaning

[1] Halford E. Luccock, *In the Minister's Workshop*, p. 11.

in it. The maelstrom of the immediate whirl goes around too fast for any steady view of past or future. In John Galsworthy's *The White Monkey* the young writer, Michael, looking at his contemporaries, recognized that "they were all restless—all the people he knew. They dashed and sputtered and skidded and rushed by like motorcycles." And Michael's wife, looking at a manuscript of his, handed it back to him with the cry: "This is exactly like life, Michael. It just rushes. It doesn't dwell on anything long enough to mean anything anywhere." Into such pathetic restlessness as that must life disintegrate when there are no great certainties on which its change and confusion can come to rest.

But then one takes up the Bible—the Bible in its great sweep of time through Old Testament and New, the Bible that is the revelation of Him with whom a "day is . . . as a thousand years, and a thousand years as one day."

1. First of all, the preacher who is to be the Bible's true interpreter needs to contemplate the long drama of history. History in the full meaning of that word is more than a list of unrelated events, which is all that some ancient records are. The chronicles of a people may be fragmentary traditions strung together without a recognition of their over-all significance. The facts of the past may be regarded as hidden lakes in a half-known country might be regarded by the explorer who comes upon them one by one. So far as he has seen, they are separate and unrelated; and so far as many early chroniclers have seen, the events of the human story lie similarly like isolated springs with no connection that brings them all together in the whole terrain of thought. But history in the great sense is the perception of facts and forces not as separate, but as belonging to a vaster unity that waits to be

80

understood. What might have appeared as self-contained lakes become revealed as parts of a far-spread system. The profound historian, like the explorer and geographer of a continent, becomes aware of immense controls that unify what at first seemed separate, as the slope of a continental watershed draws innumerable streams in one direction. All of these are tributaries making their way toward a deeper channel, until they come together into an ultimate unity of meaning as in a river running to the sea.

That is the kind of history which the Bible presents. And one needs to open his eyes to the wide sweep of its interpretation before he can understand its details.

It is, of course, not a survey of the records of the whole human race. It has to do with the particular people of Israel. But in the history of that people we can see with concentrated understanding the drama of time and human character. Here is the pageant of a people moving past the landmarks of age after age, and life goes on while forms and institutions rise and flourish and fall away.

This history of Israel, as the Old Testament presents it, begins with Abraham. A very small beginning it might have seemed at first. Moved by an unseen compulsion which the unspiritual man could not have understood, he came from Ur of the Chaldeans into the distant country that was his land of promise. "I will make of thee a great nation" said what was to him the divine voice speaking in his soul. But there was not much sign of a great nation in this lonely adventurer of the spirit who pitched his tents now here, now there. According to Gen. 12:10 famine at one time drove Abraham into Egypt, and thought stands arrested at the contrast which those words suggest. In the Nile valley civilization had been developing for centuries. Already the pyramids were old. The

81

Pharaohs had built or would build the colossal temples at Thebes and Karnak, and set up the huge statues of themselves that proclaimed their wealth and power. In the Valley of Kings they would be buried with splendor of color, jewels, and gold in tombs so massive and majestic that supposedly they would be inviolate. Against such a background how insignificant a figure like Abraham could have seemed! He could have lived and died unnoticed, while the glory of Egypt endured. But the temples and palaces which the Pharaohs built are ruins by the banks of the immemorial river and their tombs were robbed and desecrated. The one-time glory of Egypt has so long since gone back to the near oblivion of the drifting desert that the might of her kings seems only an echo down the distant corridors of almost forgotten years. It is difficult for men of this later time, accustomed to think of the seats of influence as established in very different lands, to realize that it was once there in Egypt that all the highest flowering of human life was centered.

The drama of the history which is written in the Bible moves on. Egypt sank into secondary significance. In the East great new empires arose. First it was Babylonia, then Assyria with its capital at Nineveh on the Tigris, then Babylonia again, then Persia under Cyrus. In museums today stand fragments of the huge sculpture and memorial inscriptions by which the Babylonian conquerors published what they thought would be their everlasting power. There they confront us still, the hugh brawny and bearded warriors, the iron chariots and the horses of their far-spreading armies. It seemed in their day that nothing could ever overthrow them. Yet they are gone, and their inscriptions are only puzzles for the archaeologists or curiosities for us to gaze at in the dead exhibits of a world which once was and is no more.

Still the pageant of the history that is linked with the Bible moves across the stage of the centuries. Alexander the Great led his Greek phalanxes into the east and established almost a world dominion, which crumbled with his death. The ships of Carthage swept the Mediterranean, and Hannibal led its armies across the Alps; but Carthage was blotted out at length by the other power that ended the struggle between them with the implacable cry *Carthago delenda est!* So came the mighty ascendancy of Rome. There in the imperial city was established the authority that ruled the world, and across the earth the tread of the Roman legions echoed. When the last book in the Bible was written, Rome was still regnant; but in the Bible already, particularly in that great flaming book of Revelation, were the prophecies that grew out of the moral certainty that Rome too should fall.

The final pages of the Bible were written some eighteen hundred years ago, but as a witness to the continuing drama of human life it was not finished then. In its translations out of the original tongues into the languages of new nations— by Jerome, Ulfilas, Luther, Wycliffe, Tyndale, Coverdale, the revisers of 1611, and many others in the long succession— the Bible has entered into the warp and woof of human thought through the Dark Ages that followed the fall of Rome, through the medieval period, and straight down into modern times. Its immense and inescapable testimony has confronted the thought and conscience of men while other earthly empires—such as Egypt, Babylon, Assyria, and Rome before them—have arisen, flourished, and gone their way. And what is it that the Bible compels the thoughtful to remember? It is this: that man as a spirit is more important

83

than anything which a particular generation may build and try to identify with the permanent values of man. It is well for that to be understood. Each age is tempted to think that it is the focus and the climax of existence. Every generation is tempted to assume that it is the be-all and the end-all of the human drama. An existing order looks back condescendingly upon the great civilizations of the past and accepts as an indifferent matter of fact that they did rise and blossom and fade and fall into dust, and that such, of course, was the way of life's preliminaries, but that we have arrived at permanence. The structures that we have built will not suffer from the touch of time. The particular institutions, the social and economic order which we have fashioned, must not be called in question. Life must be fixed within the conditions of living where we have put men and told them to remain content. But it is not so. The awesome and the humbling story of many nations as reflected in the Bible makes us confess that it is not so. What we need to remember is that nothing is permanent except the permanent unrest of the human spirit, which because it began in a spark of God, must challenge every partial embodiment of its hopes. The Bible makes us understand that no age, however rich and opulent and cultured, can arrogantly rest upon its own accomplishments. Always the question is: Is it recognizing the everlasting hunger of man's spirit? Is it making possible for him a world of thought, of desire, and of aspiration that is increasingly more spacious? If so, then we still belong in the ongoing current of life. If not, then life will break through our discarded forms and split the shell of our insufficient order and move toward some unknown and awful chapter in a destiny ordained of God.

2. "In a destiny ordained of God"—those words take us across the threshold of the second great realization that must come to the man who would know the Bible and help his people know it. The Bible not only reflects the long drama of life; it reveals that which gives this drama meaning. Against the moving and vanishing pageant of human existence, it lifts the eternal background of the reality of God. It is this that makes the Old Testament and its climax in the Gospels supreme among the histories of the earth. It is this that gives it a richness of value beyond that of any other record. It would be difficult to discover any element of enduring worth for the human spirit which has come out of the cruel paganisms of Babylon and Assyria. There *have* been some noble contributions to the thought of mankind from ancient Egypt, and a greater and more precious legacy of philosophy and created beauty from Greece, and of order and justice from the genius in government of Rome. But the emphasis in Israel was different. The great figures of the Old Testament did not build pyramids and raise monuments to their own achievements. They did not produce great art. They did not write comedies or tragedies to be enacted on the stage. The one area of their supreme concern was the transcendent fact of God and his relationship to men. It was in this light that all life was viewed, both the life of individuals and that of the people as a whole.

He who knows the Bible, therefore, begins to see life in its ultimate dimensions. He will not have to discount or disvalue ideas of truth and awareness of beauty which come to him from other sources. But these are not enough. There is a holiness of truth and a beauty of holiness which dawns upon a man most surely when he is led by the Bible into a realized consciousness of God.

That will not arise out of argument or theory. It will not come to the man who goes to the Bible only on sporadic hunts for a text to meet the emergency of next Sunday's sermon. It must come instead out of quietness—the quietness of a brooding meditation. "Be still, and know that I am God." Think of the vision at Bethel, until in hushed desire your soul reaches out toward the ladder set up on earth to heaven, with the angels of God ascending and descending it. Stand with Moses before the burning bush, and listen to the voice that speaks again out of its mystic flame. Go with Isaiah into the Temple to behold the Lord high and lifted up, until even to us also may come some echo of the chanting of the seraphim, "Holy, holy, holy, is the Lord of hosts; the whole earth is full of his glory." Or gaze into the vastness of the sky, as did Amos in the wilderness of Tekoa—Amos who at first was "no prophet, neither . . . a prophet's son"—and "seek him that maketh the seven stars and Orion, and turneth the shadow of death into the morning, and maketh the day dark with night; that calleth for the waters of the sea, and poureth them out upon the face of the earth: The Lord is his name." Within those vast spaces of the Bible the man who stands in reverence and wonder breathes an atmosphere that is not of this earth. The heaven above him is more exalted; the horizon of his hope and faith is bright with the radiance of a wider dawn.

John Henry Jowett was one who brought into his preaching in the early 1900's a luminousness of spirit that is increasingly needed in this shadowed century. Through him there shone a conviction of God that was ineffable, which yet the humblest man could feel and be the better for it. It was the light that never was on land or sea—the light that was also in Phillips Brooks and in other great preachers who have first of all been great souls. Of both Jowett and Brooks it was true that they had dwelt continually with and in the Bible. So there could happen in the realm of the spirit what Jowett illustrated in *The Preacher: His Life and Work:*

I once called upon a cobbler whose home was in a little seaside town in the North of England. He worked alone in an exceedingly tiny room. I asked him if he did not sometimes feel oppressed by the imprisonment of his little chamber. "Oh, no," he replied, "if any feelings of that sort begin I just open this door!" And he opened a door [that] . . . gave him a glorious view of the sea! The little room was glorified in its vast relations. To the cobbler's bench there came the suggestion of the infinite.[2]

And Jowett continued:

I think this expresses my conception of our ministry as we encounter men and women in their daily lot. We are to open that door and let in the inspiration of the Infinite! We are to go about skilfully relating everything to God:—the lowliest toil, the most unwelcome duty, the task that bristles with difficulty, the grey disappointment, the black sorrow,—we are to open the door, and let in upon them the light of the infinite purpose and the warm inspirations of eternal love.[3]

The only man who can thus be "relating everything to God" is the man who has steeped himself in the Bible. Only *he* can have said of him what was said of Thomas Binney: "He seemed to look at the horizon rather than at an enclosed field, or a local landscape. He had a marvellous way of connecting every subject with eternity past and with eternity to come."

3. Thus the Bible, which reflects the long drama of human

[2] Pp. 195-96. Used by permission of Harper & Bros.
[3] *Ibid.,* p. 196.

history in general, is centrally concerned with one particular history—the history of the people whose supreme belief it was that all their life was guided and determined by the hand of God. This history of Israel would have superlative interest even if it were only a record of the past. But it is much more than a record of the past; it is the history of a continuing faith that moves into the living present. It belongs not only to Jewry, but to Christendom. The New Testament comes directly out of the Old. Faith in Christ has its complete significance only when it is seen as the fulfillment of the hopes and longings of patriarchs and prophets and of all in the long succession that lifted their eyes to God. That is why the man who is to preach the Christian gospel should know not only some of the Bible, but the Bible as a whole.

The early Christians had the sure conviction that they were the new Israel. No one can read the Gospel of Matthew, the speeches of Peter in the book of Acts, Paul's letter to the Romans or the letter to the Hebrews, without seeing how vivid that conviction was. So in a great, true sense the Christian Church is the new Israel now—new in the light of the revelation that was given in Jesus Christ, but inheriting and transmitting that age-old witness to God and to God's purpose in Israel's history of which the Old Testament tells. When a man remembers this, then into his thought and his preaching there can come a new spaciousness and power. For he will not be seeing his people as some little group that happened at an accidental moment to form themselves into an ephemeral congregation. He will see them as part of the ecclesia which God called and through which God has been acting ever since Abraham went out from Ur of the Chaldeans to seek "for a city which hath foundations, whose builder and maker is God."

88

Consider what that history which began with Abraham is. It is the story not primarily of what a people desired and might have done, but rather of what God's unwearying purpose wrought in them. It is the story of the Exodus and of Sinai, of hardships in the wilderness and of entrance at last into the Promised Land; hope and disappointment, bitterness of defeat and exile, but through it all a far-reaching purpose that nothing could defeat. To Abraham, adventurer of the spirit, was given the promise, "I will . . . make thy name great; and thou shalt be a blessing." With him and his descendants, according to the faith that has kept Israel indestructible through centuries that have seen empires rise and fall, God had made an everlasting covenant. In the strength of that covenant the people oppressed in Egypt cried to God out of their distress. Moses was raised up as their deliverer, to confront Pharaoh, to gird the people in the Passover, to find the perilous road to freedom across the Red Sea. Slowly a nation came into being—a nation whose distinguishing mark was that, in spite of lapses into unfaithfulness and many failures, it carried the conviction that its whole life must be a witness to the saving act of God. As in the voice of Joshua, its leaders were continually reaffirming, "As for me and my house, we will serve the Lord." The child Samuel became the symbol of the response which something deep within this people's soul continually desired to echo—"Speak, Lord; for thy servant heareth." David is idealized as the representation of rulership because in his central purpose he was considered to be a man "after [God's] own heart." And steadily the conception of God's will and purpose widened. Elijah defied Jezebel and her pagan priests of Baal and confronted Ahab at the gate of Naboth's vineyard—intrepid spokesman for the God of righteousness and champion of the common man.

Amos, Hosea, Isaiah, Jeremiah, proclaimed the sovereignty of God, to whose justice all classes within a people and all nations of the earth are equally accountable, and by whose mercy alone their life can be redeemed. And when Jerusalem fell and there followed the bitter years of exile, still there burned the unquenched flames of faith that the "everlasting God, the Lord, the Creator of the ends of the earth, fainteth not, neither is weary," and that through him Israel, or a remnant of it, should forever be a witness to his saving grace.

In the early 1900's there was created and staged in Europe and America a dramatic pageant called *The Eternal Road.* In the foreground was a group of men and women belonging to the synagogue. Under the shadow of continual danger and the threat of pogroms, still they met to celebrate the immemorial Jewish feasts, to listen to the reading of the law and the prophets, to hear again their history. Back of them, across the breadth of a vast stage was silently enacted the history of which they heard: the tense Passover on the night of the Exodus from Egypt, the crossing of the Red Sea, the giving of the law, and so on through the long record of peril, and of patience, and of the unconquerable courage that followed a hope that was in God alone. And behind that pageant, and higher up, there was a background as of heaven, where in a glimpsed mystery were ranks of angels whose watching guardianship gave eternal meaning to the people who walked upon their eternal road.

What has that to say, then, to the Christian preacher and to the congregation to whom he would interpret the fullness of the Bible? It is this: that the foundations of his message are as deep and old as Old Testament time, and that on those foundations he is to build what is more wonderful and new. Christianity inherits what is great in Judaism: its identity as

90

a people of the covenant, the dignity that belongs to every individual because he is part of the unbroken fellowship of redemption. But it adds to that a mightier and more radiant realization of what redemption is. The Old Testament revelation which Jesus rejoiced in and which he constantly exalted comes to its climax in him—in what he taught and in what he meant to his disciples, in his crucifixion and his resurrection, and in the new fellowship of the Church of which he is the Lord. So the Old Testament is seen in an ultimate perspective. This is what the purpose of God for the covenant people was forever meant to be—life redeemed by the recognition that its sin is so dreadful that it can crucify the Redeemer when he comes but that God's love thus crucified will still come back to save. When this message is preached to a Christian congregation, a new sense of greatness under God can come to all those who have been tempted to think of themselves as insignificant and of the church they belong to as an ordinary, uninspired thing. They will begin to perceive themselves as links in an eternal destiny. In them and by them God may carry forward what he began in Israel—the calling of a people who would be different and would make the life around them different, because he would take hold of them and let his spirit express itself in what they are and do. And it is God not only as he was known in the laws of Sinai who calls. It is God as revealed in the love of Jesus who would be saying through every Christian preacher to wistful people in the pews, "I have chosen you."

SUGGESTIONS FOR SUPPLEMENTARY READING

Blackwood, Andrew W. *Preaching from the Bible*. New York and Nashville: Abingdon Press, 1941.

Bowie, Walter Russell. *The Bible*. New York: Association Press: 1940.
————. *The Story of the Bible*. New York and Nashville: Abingdon Press, 1934.
Dodd, C. H. *The Bible Today*. New York: The Macmillan Co., 1947.
Interpreter's Bible, The. New York and Nashville: Abingdon Press. Especially Vols. I and VII.
Nelson, Lawrence E. *Our Roving Bible*. New York and Nashville: Abingdon Press, 1945.
Roach, Corwin C. *Preaching Values in the Bible*. Chicago: Wilcox & Follett Co., 1946.
Soares, Theodore G. *The Origins of the Bible*. New York: Harper & Bros., 1941.
Swaim, J. Carter. *Right and Wrong Ways to Use the Bible*. Philadelphia: Westminster Press, 1953.

CHAPTER SIX

Preaching from the Old Testament

THE MAN WHO knows his whole Bible will have no doubt of the truth which Charles R. Brown expressed when he wrote that "the land of Scripture is a good land. It is a land of hills and valleys that drinketh water of the rain of heaven. And it is a land of endless variety . . . ; a land where thou mayest eat bread without scarceness and not lack any good thing." [1]

But it is a fact that men who acknowledge the richness of the Bible in general may yet have an inadequate recognition of the value for their preaching of that great part of it which is included in the Old Testament. Some men neglect the Old Testament unthinkingly because they are not awake to its vital interest, and others neglect it deliberately because they hold that they must try to preach nothing but the saving gospel, and the fully saving gospel is not there. But indifference to the Old Testament for either one of those reasons can be a mistake that will restrict the scope of preaching and rob it of the spaciousness and power which the great preachers have possessed. For the New Testament grows directly out of the Old. It was the God of the patriarchs and the prophets

[1] *Op. cit.*, p. 40.

93

whom Jesus called "my Father and your Father." It was of the great Old Testament revelations of the law of God for human life that he said, "One jot or one tittle shall in no wise pass . . . till all be fulfilled." Therefore the man who wants to bring to his people the full sweep of God's truth as it relates to their own needs can often turn with happy expectancy to the Old Testament for his inspiration.

In doing so—let it be remembered at the outset—he must have these clear principles to guide him:

1. He should be honest.

Is a preacher likely to be anything else? it may be asked. To which it must be answered that the preacher, being fallible and imperfect, even though he might never want to be actually dishonest, is nevertheless liable to temptations that make him twist the truth. He can twist the truth by refusing to follow it in the direction where he knows that prevailing opinion does not want to go. Too many men in the pulpit, generation after generation, have denounced new discoveries about the universe, about the origin and history of man, about the Bible, because they could not bring themselves to face the painful and unpopular process of breaking up old, comfortable patterns of thought and adjusting their minds, and their people's minds, to the new realities. Even when they have had the uneasy feeling that ideas the conservatives were afraid of might prove to be the truth, they have tried to drown that uneasiness by being all the more vehement about what was supposed to be believed. The occasions for that kind of conflict change with the times, but in one form or another they recur. Any preacher about to write a sermon may see in his mind's eye some influential parishioner who would be offended unless he smothers or softens what he really thinks, and little by little he may lose the victory which comes to the man whom people in the long run will respect and listen to because they know that he is sincere.

2. He must be informed.

The Bible, and the Old Testament particularly, belongs in a historical setting which must be studied to be understood. Nobody can rightly interpret Genesis and Exodus without having learned all he can about why and how those books were written, and what great spiritual insights shine everlastingly through their whole record, over and above whatever critical analysis may say as to this or that factual detail. Nobody can preach effectively on such books as Joshua, Judges, Samuel, Kings—no, nor on the wide emotional sweep of the book of Psalms—without getting a right perspective between their perception of the will of God and the human passions that were like smoke through which men could not see completely. And certainly no one can interpret the message of the prophets without knowing the order in which they came, the particular conditions which challenged them to prophesy, and the living impact of what they said. Preachers who have had no opportunity for scholastic training have been made instruments of the Spirit within the limits of their knowledge, but that gives no alibi to the man who might have knowledge but instead is lazily ignorant. "God may indeed use the foolishness of preaching, but we are under obligation to see that it is not more foolish than it need be." [2]

3. The preacher must have common sense.

That is to say, he must have the judgment and the discipline of mind that will keep him from the exaggerated fancies and

[2] Herbert H. Farmer, *The Servant of the Word*, p. 31.

the rhetorical flourishes which the best of his listeners may find ridiculous. Frederick Lewis Allen once drew a picture of this kind of preaching—a picture that for all its good humor was at the same time devastating in its satire. He called his article "How to Preach a Sermon." He wrote:

Suppose your text (from the David and Goliath chapter to which I referred) is "Thy servant kept his father's sheep." Amplify this. Tell just how David did it, or how you think he must have done it, or might possibly have done it. With all that active work in the field, a boy like David must have had to keep in good physical condition, mustn't he? Well, there you are on the brink of a boy scout sermon, or perhaps one on prohibition. And we may be very sure that David must have been gentle with the sheep, mayn't we? (There's your kindness to animals lead, if you want it.) And can't we imagine him coming back every night to Jesse and his brothers and telling them, as they sat about the supper table, how many lions and bears he had seen that day; and doesn't this (if you like) give us an inspiring idea of what family life might be like right here and now in America if it weren't for divorce and companionate marriage and things? If you amplify a text like this in the right way you can make a smooth start toward almost any subject under the heavens (those same heavens, I might add, which David sat and watched as he faithfully kept his sheep).[3]

That kind of amplifying can indeed make a smooth start in some direction, but it leads to nothing more edifying than a new act in a homiletical circus.

4. The preacher should be constructive.

The need for honesty was remembered first of all. The servant of the God of truth will not preach what he does not believe or conceal what he does believe. But that does not mean that his business is with negations, though some

[3] Used by permission of Harper & Bros.

callous and self-important little persons in the pulpit seem to think so. A congregation will have little use for the man who likes to create a sensation by telling them what is not so; they want to hear about what *is* so and on which they can build their lives. If a man confronts them with the necessity of clearing away old ideas, they want to be sure that it is in order to build something larger and better in their place. The duty of the preacher is that which Henry Sloane Coffin made plain in one of his unforgettable illustrations. A time came when the old red-brick building that was the Grand Central Station in New York became inadequate. The growing tides of life it served required that it be replaced by something greater. What to do, then? Stop the railroads from running, or shift them somewhere else? But that was impossible. The old building had to be demolished and the new one built over and around it while the immense coming and going of the railroads continued uninterrupted. And that was accomplished. The tens of thousands of railroad travelers went through temporary passageways of rough planks; plaster and dust were in the air and noise and confusion all about. But people could take those things uncomplainingly because they knew the destruction was a necessary condition to something nobler that was being built. And so it is with all true preaching. People can accept the uncomfortable process of having their outgrown ideas broken up if they see that the end will be not a lessening of their spiritual life but a creative enlargement of what life is and what it leads to.

5. So the preacher can be confident.

He can know that in a vital interpretation of the Bible he can bring to his people much that will enrich their minds and souls. Frederick Lewis Allen, in his whimsical treatment of

97

the verse about David showed how a preacher's irresponsible license can make a sermon laughable. But the very words which his imagined preacher can exaggerate have a central suggestion which the genuine preacher can rejoice in. David daring to face Goliath because he could remember what happened when he kept his father's sheep—that is no mere springboard for artificial talk. It is a reminder of a clear truth —the truth of the power of previous faithfulness. Because David knew that by God's help he had met his lesser tests, he knew now that he could meet the greater one. And so repeatedly out of the Old Testament comes the straight, sure message that has directly to do with life; and a man can proclaim it with a boldness which nothing can dismay.

So much for the spirit in which the Old Testament should be approached. Now what can be found there for preaching.

Open the pages of the Bible no further than the first and second chapters. According to the profound spiritual awareness which they embody, God who alone was "in the beginning" created the universe and "saw that it was good." As the crown of creation he made man, that in his human spirit he might reflect the heavenly Spirit. But in the story of Adam and Eve in the Garden there is the everlasting dramatization of the fact that human self-will and disobedience make their fateful breach with God and go out into spiritual exile. Biblical interpretations change with growing knowledge, and readers of the book of Genesis are not likely now to think of Adam and Eve as precisely dated and particular persons who can be put down as having lived in 4004 B.C.—which is exactly the way they are put down at the top of the printed page in many older editions of the King James Bible, according to the confident chronology of Archbishop Ussher. That literalism is

98

not needed to make the story of what happened in the Garden eternally significant. Here is a profound insight into human life in its relationship to God. And all the Old Testament is the vivid exemplification of the aspects of that relationship: on the one hand, the everlasting outreach of God's holiness and his redeeming purpose; and on the other hand, the infinitely varied response of human souls, sometimes turning wistfully back toward God, sometimes turning away into more deliberate rebellion. Not only as part of an ancient story but as a symbol of living fact that is forever contemporary is the Cain whose rebellion makes him a "fugitive and a vagabond," and equally contemporary can be the desire reflected in an Enoch who "walked with God."

So the first and most vivid value of the Old Testament for the preacher may be in the figures it portrays—these figures, so many and so varied, that represent the everlasting tension between the call of God and the drag of evil.

Sometimes the moral and spiritual significance breaks through in just a sudden hint, sometimes it stands unmistakably revealed in a longer story, but in either case the extraordinary power of the Old Testament is that it does make us instinctively say, "That is true of human life, and it is true for me." Out of the multitude of such Old Testament suggestions consider only a typical few.

Noah is described as a "righteous man, blameless in his generation" (Gen. 6:9 R.S.V.); but in Gen. 9:21 we come upon the startling description of Noah disgracefully drunk. Here is incitement to reflection on the circumstances that can make a good man temporarily go to pieces. According to the story Noah had borne himself with extraordinary steadiness and courage as long as he had something important to do. He had built the Ark and got his family and the animals into it

99

and kept it afloat during the flood, and at last he had landed it on solid ground; so now what he did might not seem to matter, and besides he was sick of all the long strain of responsibility. Perhaps accumulated irritations were breaking out. Men do get drunk from causes such as that, and as the problem of drunkenness is as continuous as human history, it is worth while to let this spark of suggestion in the Noah story kindle consideration as to how and why it happens.

Among the unforgettable figures in the book of Genesis is Esau. At first glance he seems a far more attractive and promising person than his brother Jacob: the hearty, out-of-doors man; impulsive and yet easygoing; affectionate, easily satisfied, and only belatedly roused to anger. Yet it was Esau whom the King James translation of the Epistle to the Hebrews describes as a "profane" man, meaning a man who in sheer carelessness could treat contemptuously the holy possibilities of life. Hungry for Joseph's pottage, wanting what he wanted when he wanted it, concerned with the obvious and immediate benefit, why should he bother about his "birthright"? That was intangible, and if it was important, he could think about it tomorrow; anyway it did not seem to be any use now, today. So he bargained off the birthright for the desired thing at hand. How subtly and how frequently that same error may be repeated!—in the young man who lets some opportunity for quick material gain win him away from an idealistic career which at first had beckoned him, in the good-natured but slack-principled man in politics who thinks that getting for people the favors they want is more realistic and more rewarding than guarding the birthright of a community's civic honor.

Or look at other figures in the early Old Testament books that represent lives—or the moments that may come in any life—when God's meaning for them is lost. There is the ignominy of the excuse that Aaron tried to make to Moses when he, Aaron, had yielded to the crowd's demand and had made an image for them to worship: "You know the people, that they are set on evil. For they said to me, 'Make us gods.' . . . And I said to them, 'Let any who have gold take it off'; so they gave it to me, and I threw it into the fire, and there came out this calf." (Exod. 32:22-24 R.S.V.) It was the people's fault, even the calf's fault! Somebody else started the wrong idea, and the evil thing just happened. Why blame me? said Aaron. And are there no descendants of Aaron now?

Or, from a little further along in the Old Testament, consider Samson. Here was a man who had magnificent strength and courage in the rougher fields of life, but no strength on the inner arena where the issues of character are at stake. And because he was weak there, ultimately he was weak everywhere. The tragedy of his life is summed up in one poignant sentence of description of what happened after he had yielded to the enticements of Delilah. "She said, 'The Philistines are upon you, Samson!' And he awoke from his sleep, and said, 'I will go out as at other times, and shake myself free.' And he did not know that the Lord had left him." (Judg. 16:20 R.S.V.) He did not know! There is the pathos of the awful fact that a man's sins may make him powerless before disaster and doom him like Samson to be chained in the prison of the forces he ought to have overcome.

But a deeper tragedy is in the story of Saul. Look at him as he was first: handsome, tall in stature and in spirit, brave and magnanimous, superbly fitted to be an instrument in the hand of God. Such an instrument it seemed that he would truly be. Then he became obsessed by one poisonous emotion, his jealousy of David, which gradually infected and

LINCOLN BIBLE INSTITUTE

101

overcame the great part of him which had been gallant and good. All his energies were turned now not to the service of God but passionately to what he thought was his own protection. At length there came this agonizing cry: "I am in great distress; for the Philistines are warring against me, and God has turned away from me and answers me no more" (I Sam. 28:15 R.S.V.). Then on the final battlefield at Mount Gilboa, with the Philistines triumphant and his own kingdom shattered, he fell on his own sword and died. So in that physical death he enacted what was a parable of his spiritual death, and became a symbol of what may be a recurrent tragedy—the tragedy of the potentially noble man who by some abandonment of his ideals falls upon his own perverted possibilities and turns what ought to have been his sword of service into a sword of suicide.

Such are some of the shadowed figures in the Old Testament. But then there were those on whom and in whom there was a brighter light. Abraham, in Ur of the Chaldeans, heard the voice from God that bade him leave the environment and the associations to which he might have clung; and "he went out," says the Epistle to the Hebrews, "not knowing where he was to go" (11:8 R.S.V.). Strange description for a life that was to be significant! We tend to think that the consequential man is the hard-headed practical man who, before he attempts anything, knows exactly what he is doing. Abraham was not like that. He was the kind of man who cannot see far along the road on which he adventures because it is too high a road for its end to be visible from the levels where men start. He cannot fully know where he is going because he lives in the strength of tomorrow and not only within the limits of today. So one is led to contemplate Abraham's motives, the length and difficulty and sometimes

102

the disappointments of the way on which he went, and then finally the strange fact of the achievement which seemed to be no achievement. For this man who looked for the "city which has foundations, whose builder and maker is God" (Heb. 11:10 R.S.V.)—what city did he ever attain more stable than the roving tents in which he dwelt? None, it might appear. Yet as a matter of fact, the story of his life has created among men a center of faith and inspiration more enduring than any visible city; and because of it any man today who hears the call of an ideal too great for him to prove can follow it more bravely and with better hope.

So is it also with the story of Joseph, the "dreamer." A great vision of the possibilities of life may seem nothing but illusion, as Joseph's imagination seemed to his scornful brothers. And it might have been no better than illusion if he had not had the moral faithfulness to live up to it, through the bitter hurt of his brothers' malice, through the temptation in Potiphar's house, through false accusation and imprisonment. But this man who would not sin against God nor against his high estimate of his own soul could see at last that the worst which had happened to him was not accidental evil, but the very hand of God overruling evil to bring his life to its fulfillment. Whenever any man is tempted to think that what he has believed in is beaten down by the harsh facts of his existence, he can remember Joseph.

Or suppose that one who has to preach is brought face to face with the problem of why it is that God may let the way ahead seem so long and hard and discouraging for the person who has truly wanted to dedicate himself to some unselfish service. It may be that a minister's own work in his parish has brought him to this distress. Why should it be that there is so much misunderstanding, perhaps even misrepresentation,

103

and plain stubborn resistance to the best he has tried to do? Or he may be thinking of some fine person in his congregation or his community who in social work, in business circles, or in public affairs has dared to advance the new ideals which the general conscience knows it ought to follow, and has been met by the angry mutterings of those who say, "The old was good enough; you let us alone!" At such a moment one can turn again to the Old Testament and read the heroic story of Moses, who left the advantages of Pharaoh's house and went out to lead a people toward what he knew could be their Promised Land. From that story one can understand that the victorious lives are those which can go forward exactly as Moses did through long days when the people around him either disbelieved what he believed in or were so fainthearted and feeble that they wanted to turn back anyway —and when the only way the leader could keep steady was to shut his eyes to human opposition and endure "as seeing him who is invisible" (Heb. 11:27). So out of the Old Testament pages comes again a message for life in every time— that greatness lies in laying hold of the high commission and carrying it through with that steadiness which God alone makes possible. Thus after the example of Moses a man today may be enabled to say of himself what Miles Coverdale during the danger of his translating the Bible said, "Therefore, when I was instantly required to do my task, though I could not do it as well as I would, I thought it yet my duty to do my best, and that with a good will."

Such then are some of the figures of the Old Testament which can strike the spark of man's imagination when he asks himself, "What shall I preach?" And how easily the list can be lengthened: Isaac, the lesser son of the great father, who yet became an example of the quiet virtues; Joshua,

Caleb, Gideon, the stalwarts who were stronger than the crowd; Jonathan, truehearted and heroic, almost the only character in the Old Testament on whom there is no stain; Nehemiah, who rebuilt the Holy City; Ruth, with her unswerving loyalty; Esther, who took her life in her hands to save her people. And it is not only from the conspicuous figures that inspirations come. Often some almost incidental mention may throw its sudden shaft of light upon suggested truth. In Gen. 24:27 Eliezer, Abraham's servant, on his errand to find a bride for Isaac thanked God for the divine help that had not failed him. "I am on the right road," he said —in the phrase of the Smith-Goodspeed American translation—or, as the King James Version puts it, "I being in the way, the Lord led me." How revealing that is of the double element that must be in any spiritual enterprise for it to gain fulfillment. Not only must it look to God for guidance; it must be on its way with the kind of alert activity and obedience which God can guide.

Or look at those words in Gen. 35:8, so unobtrusive that they are like Wordsworth's

> . . . violet by a mossy stone,
> Half hidden from the eye!

"Deborah Rebekah's nurse died"—this is all, except that she was buried under what was called the "oak of weeping." Yet in those terse words is there not a whole world of poignant associations? The person obscure and humble and to history unimportant may be one who has brought, or brings, precious values that are mourned when they are gone. Who cannot remember some nurse whose selfless devotion has blessed the life of a home by her quiet spirit?—such as the one to whom

105

Robert Louis Stevenson dedicated his *Child's Garden of Verses* as "from her boy," in gratitude

> For the long nights you lay awake
> And watched for my unworthy sake.

How much of the sweetness and security of all life is due to the little people whose uncalculating kindness comes to us in a measure of which we are unworthy!

Sermons from texts like these in the Old Testament are not the ultimate message. They may not seem at first to touch the profound matters of the faith. But they may be a good place to begin. Men will be more aware both of the meaning of the gospel and of their need for it if they have considered first some of the plain facts of human character in the realism with which the Old Testament presents them. For here one can see men of like passions and like possibilities with ourselves, involved in the same struggles, faced with the same critical choices between unregenerate lives and the leading of God. The characters of the Old Testament are not only Abraham or Isaac or Esau or Saul or David: they are everyman, and they belong to every time.

Besides the narratives about persons other parts of the Old Testament similarly belong to every time. The forms of speech may reflect another age, but what is dealt with is never outdated. No change of circumstance invalidates the shrewd wisdom of the book of Proverbs or makes the Psalms less wonderful in the everlasting emotions that sound through them as on the strings of a great harp—joy and sorrow, praise and penitence, the awful abasement of the *De Profundis*, and the glory of the *Jubilate*. The gray and weary sense of meaninglessness which has fallen like a fog on much of the twentieth-century world can see its own mood reflected in Ecclesiastes; the continual problem of life's injustices is wrestled with in Job; and what the Spaniard Unamuno voiced as a message in the face of tragedy, "May God deny you peace but give you glory," [4] is an echo of what the greater prophets said and what they still are saying to all who read the Bible. With that last reference the thought of the man who is to preach is brought directly into touch with one of the mightiest stimulations that can come from the Old Testament: namely, the significance of the prophets. Among the prophets some were greater than others, but the whole succession of them stands up above the ordinary levels of history like towering mountains of which even the least was great. No one can look at them without feeling his spirit affected by their loftiness—and that in a double aspect.

For in the first place the prophets of whom most is recorded were men of massive character. They compel attention because of what they did and what they dared. There was nothing tame about them, no languid atmosphere as of the flat plains where ordinary life may be content. The great winds of passionate contention blew upon them, and like the high mountains they drew the clouds from which thunder and lightning break. To think of the prophets is to have something vivid and exciting to preach about. They made history, not only for their own times but for all time, by the influences they set in motion.

First, and among the most formidable, consider Elijah. In that man's conviction and his courage there was let loose the spirit that increasingly in human history has "scattered the

---

[4] *The Tragic Sense of Life in Men and in Peoples* (New York: The Macmillan Co., 1921).

proud in the imagination of their hearts, . . . put down the mighty from their seats, and exalted them of low degree." Elijah standing up alone against the corruptions that had come to Israel with Jezebel, Elijah challenging the whole company of the priests of Baal, Elijah confronting Ahab at the gate of Naboth's vineyard and calling down God's judgment on this king who had committed vile injustice against a common man—*there* is one of the fountainheads of the moral force that ever since then has been on the side of social righteousness.

Or see again in imagination that scene in Bethel when Amos, with no outward badge of authority but with the awful fire that blazed out of his soul, faced the kept priest Amaziah, asserted the prophethood that had come to him in the desert silences, and against the sins of a whole civilization dared to hurl the awful judgments of "thus saith the Lord." Hosea, keeping his loyalty and his desperate hope in the face of scorn and ignominy; Isaiah, holding a people's morale together through the Assyrian peril; Jeremiah, with the far more difficult and agonizing duty of telling the terrible truth of national doom to men who spat upon him for what in their rage they counted as his treason—these were *men*, whose magnificent witness to what men can live up to is an inspiration that will live as long as there are lips to tell of it and consciences to respond.

But the prophets of course have a further importance. Not only were they heroic men; in a special sense they were God's messengers. So the prophetic books which record their preaching are a resource for all preaching. If a man has read the prophets' words with the living imagination that sees beneath the accidents of ancient time and circumstance the enduring truths with which they were on fire, then he will carry power with him as he goes into his pulpit.

He studies, for instance, the prophecies of Amos and Hosea. Some reactionary group in his community, or even individuals in his own church, may have been arguing that religion has nothing to do with public affairs and that the pulpit should mind its own business, which is saving men's souls. Amos and Hosea have their devastating answer for that sort of ignorance. Saving men's souls—yes, that was what they made their business, but it was a bigger and bolder business than pietistic complacency had ever understood. For a man really to be saved—and for a people to be saved— meant to be saved all through and in all relationships. It meant that the whole of life had to be looked at in the light of God. And that was exactly what Amos and Hosea determined should be done. People might behave themselves very properly in their customary worship, but what did they do out in their everyday world? The prophets asked that relentless question, and then they went on to give the answer—not in any pleasant generalities, but with the power of hard facts. "You . . . turn justice to wormwood, and cast down righteousness to the earth!" said Amos; and then he went on to specify exactly the kinds of sins that the rich and powerful among the people were committing: building luxurious houses with money cheated from the poor, corrupting the courts, crooked bargains in their business, rich food and drink for themselves while the common crowd went hungry. "Shall not the land tremble on this account?" Amos cried. And Hosea, indicating the same sins as Amos, summed up the situation in one scorching metaphor, when he said that the life he looked at was like a "cake not turned." One side of it was burned and dry with the exaggerated fervor of what pretended to be religion,

109

while all the other side of practical conduct was like raw dough. Who can listen to the voices of Amos and Hosea and not feel his own conception for his preaching vibrate to a mightier chord? In a century when great dark forces of protest are stirring among the peoples of the earth, and when all Christian civilization is on trial to determine whether it can give justice and freedom and a fuller life before the awful judgments of God in history may fall upon it, the words of the great prophets "are like channel-buoys anchored by God, and we shall do well to heed them now that the roar of an angry surf is in our ears." [5]

But the indictment of social sins by Amos and Hosea is only the beginning of the stimulus for preaching which the prophets furnish. Micah, with his immortal answer to "What doth the Lord require of thee?" Isaiah, with his unflinching realism and yet with his mighty hopes; Jeremiah, with his promise of a new covenant written not on stone but on men's hearts—these can forever be spiritual interpreters to every man who wants his preaching to be a pilgrimage toward truth.

Such, then, are some of the possibilities for preaching from the Old Testament. But how—it may be asked—ought the Christian preacher to relate his sermons from the Old Testament to the gospel of the New?

The answer to that question must have a double aspect. On the one hand, a preacher is mistaken if he uneasily supposes that he must get the whole kerygma, Incarnation, sacrifice on the cross, the Atonement, the Resurrection, into every Old Testament sermon. To try to do so may wrench the particular Old Testament content into an extension that does

[5] Walter Rauschenbusch, *Christianity and the Social Crisis*. (New York: The Macmillan Co., 1907), pp. 2-3.

not belong to its immediate reality. If one is dealing, for example, with the somber figure of Saul, he is dealing with a tragedy of failure which must be interpreted in terms of Saul's own time and circumstances, and not in terms of New Testament understanding. The prophecy of Amos has its terrific concentrated power because it is a blazing indictment of social sins and an unsparing judgment upon them, and a preacher blurs that emphasis if he tries to bring in at the same time a developed evangelism which is not there. The immortal encouragement which the prophet Habakkuk gives to troubled human souls lies in the fact that he dared to question God, and that when he stood upon his watchtower and trusted that the "righteous shall live by his faith," he was holding heroically to a light of hope shining in what was still mostly darkness. To try to introduce the whole gospel into his thought is to rob his prophecy of its unique value: namely, its kinship to those in every age who also are struggling in the dark. In other words, a sermon drawn from the Old Testament will be true to its source and will strike home to our conviction only if it gives the actual—even if limited—certainty which it contains. When the preacher supposes that he must write an explicit formulation of the New Testament gospel into that same sermon, he is turning what should be an unconfused interpretation into a palimpsest on which the original message has been obscured by what he has written over it. For a palimpsest is a "parchment or the like from which writing has been partially or completely erased to make room for another text."

Yet what has been said must not be interpreted in a way to lead to an opposite mistake. With sermons on Old Testament characters—as we have seen—the New Testament truth must not be artificially written in. But it is also true that without violating the integrity and unity of the Old Testament structure, windows can be opened toward spiritual horizons seen afar. There can be conveyed a feeling that in the whole area of Old Testament life there is a wistful incompleteness that reaches out and on to that ultimate revelation of life's meaning which is complete only in Christ. Even the greatest aspects of the Old Testament must be seen within the perspective of the New Testament fulfillment if they are to reveal all their profundity—such, for example, as the majestic conception of a covenant from God that runs through the whole Old Testament history and always was waiting for one who was to come. The love of God as Hosea began to understand it points forward to the cross. The prophecies of the Suffering Servant foreshadow the Atonement. Through all the human problems and possibilities in the Old Testament it is as though there comes a voice that cries, as Robert Browning in *Saul* has David cry:

> 'Tis the weakness in strength, that I cry for! my flesh, that
> I seek
> In the Godhead!

And then follow the words that express the intimate wonder of compassion in the gospel that hungry hearts have longed for:

> I seek and I find it. O Saul, it shall be
> A Face like my face that receives thee; a Man like to me,
> Thou shalt love and be loved by, forever: a Hand like this hand
> Shall throw open the gates of new life to thee! See the Christ stand!

SUGGESTIONS FOR SUPPLEMENTARY READING

Bowie, Walter Russell. *Great Men of the Bible.* New York: Harper & Bros., 1940.

The Interpreter's Bible. New York and Nashville. Abingdon Press, Vols. I-VI.

James, Fleming. *Personalities of the Old Testament.* New York: Chas. Scribner's Sons, 1939.

Smith, George Adam. *The Book of Isaiah.* New York: Harper & Bros., 1940.

———. *The Book of the Twelve Prophets.* New York: Harper & Bros., 1940.

Terrien, Samuel L. *The Psalms and Their Meaning for Today.* Indianapolis: Bobbs-Merrill Co., Inc., 1952.

Yates, Kyle M. *Preaching from the Prophets.* New York: Harper & Bros., 1942.

CHAPTER SEVEN

Preaching from the New Testament

FOR THE WHOLE BIBLE, but most of all for the New Testament, the man who is to preach may well thank God, in the words of one of the collects of the *Book of Common Prayer*, for having "caused all holy Scriptures to be written for our learning"; and he can go on to pray that we may "read, mark, learn, and inwardly digest them."

With regard to the New Testament, then, the first thing is to read it and to read *it*. The trouble with too many men who are going to preach is that they read books *about* it and do not half read the New Testament itself. Like Kipling's "Tomlinson" they can recite, "O this I have felt, and this I have guessed, and this I have heard men say"; but there is little that they have discovered for themselves. Yet that is the essential thing. If a man is ever genuinely to preach the New Testament, let him first live with it and listen to it with no third person in between. Let him gain an immediate consciousness of the Lord Jesus Christ before he begins to speculate about Christology. Let him in his own imagination get close enough to Paul to feel the great apostle's glowing spirit before he lets himself be immersed in what somebody wrote about Paulinism. To sit down in a quiet place and read one

114

of the Gospels straight through without interruption, and to read one of the epistles as though it were a letter sent directly to one's own self—that is the way in which the New Testament becomes a living word. And in a man's heart can grow then the confidence that he can be a preacher because he has come into contact with the realities on which the greatest preaching has always been based.

This can still be true for the man of humble spirit who says, "But when I read the New Testament, I remember how richly the gospel has been preached already. What can possibly be left that will be new for me to say?"

In one sense of course there will be nothing new—and every man can well be thankful that this is so. He does not have to invent ideas that up to now have been unheard of. The gospel is already there, with a greatness and glory that does not depend on him. He no more creates the contents of his sermons than one who is born upon a continent creates the limitless wealth of fields and rivers and prairies and mountains that stretch from sea to sea. But he can reap new harvests from the fields and explore again the rivers and find his own trails up the mountains where they soar into the sky. He can be original not in being the origin of anything, but in going to what God has given and then telling in his own way of the wonder of what he has seen and knows.

So let each man explore the New Testament with a fresh and eager mind. This does not mean of course that he will conceitedly suppose he has no need of guidance. He will want good commentaries to teach him essential facts and to keep him from going off in false directions. But he should not listen openmouthed and dumb as tourists in a cathedral often listen to some verger who recites his unchanged story. Let him learn all the best that those who know can tell him, but along

115

with that let him look with his own eyes and follow his own quickening appreciation. Let him reverently consider what the gospel has meant to others, but let him not fail to ask also, "What does it truly mean to me?" Then what he thinks and what he preaches can become not like water dipped out of a bucket, but like the stream that pours from a living spring.

A right example of this sort of approach to preaching is in a sermon preached in a homiletics section by a seminary student who knew little enough about the Bible but was on the right road to knowledge because he had a fresh desire. He began:

Once in a while a part of the scripture suddenly comes to life for us. This happens all too seldom. But recently such a passage has come alive for me. It is the parable of the wheat and the tares. First I would like to talk with you about the usual interpretation of this parable. Secondly I would like to share with you the interpretation which brought this parable to life to me.[1]

The usual interpretation, he said—or at any rate the only one he had known—was "that mankind is divided—divided into the good men whose lives are life-giving like the wheat, as opposed to the bad men whose lives are poisonous like the tares; divided into the men who will be gathered to the bosom of God, as opposed to the men who will burn in everlasting hell."

But was this really the meaning of the parable, he had asked himself—and this *all* its meaning? Or did it have another meaning, more immediate, more intimate for him? Suddenly he had an intuition that it did. "Now," he said, "I

[1] William George Frank, Virginia Theological Seminary, 1952.

have a reinterpretation of the parable, and it makes all the difference to me."

I do not see the wheat as representing churchmen and the tares as representing nonchurchmen. Rather I see that stricken field as reflective of my own stricken life—and as reflective of the lives of all of us. My own life—with its good growing like wheat and its evil like tares. My own life—on the one hand helpful and on the other nonhelpful. My own life—creative like the wheat and at the same time destructive like the tares. My own life is like this field.[2]

Then what about his aspiring to be a Christian minister? Some of his motives were genuine, he knew. But he knew too that motives are mixed, and there were some unworthy ones among the good. Why had he and other men like him come to the seminary? he asked.

Was it completely because we loved people? Or was it also a little because we wanted the prestige and adulation we have seen ministers get? Was it completely because we wanted to serve God? Or was it a little because we wanted the security that some ministers have a reputation for receiving—and a month's vacation out of the year. That would be a fine thing to tell the little old lady who comes up to us and says, "I think it is wonderful that you are dedicating your life to your Lord!" [3]

So with all those tares among the wheat, he had to face the question whether he had any right to be in the ministry at all. Then the parable brought him his answer. The Lord of the land told his workers to let the tares alone, lest in trying to root those out they uproot the wheat too. Both could grow together until the harvest, and then the wheat could be

[2] *Ibid.*
[3] *Ibid.*

sifted out. So, the lad concluded, God would deal patiently with the mixed motives in his imperfect heart. He would go on, trusting in the good seed God had put there, and trusting also that God would not let the tares spoil the harvest.

Those who know the New Testament and the history of the early Church better than he will know that his interpretation of the parable was certainly less than complete, but he had sought and found in it a living message that spoke home to his own need. And because he had caught thus a truth which was to him convincing, he carried conviction and genuine help to those who heard him preach.

The point is that here was someone who was thinking for himself. When other preachers, including more fully trained ones, do that, then many passages in the New Testament may be lifted out of the conventional familiarity which may make congregations say yawningly to themselves, "Yes, we've heard all that before." Take, for example, one of the supreme parables of Jesus. With endlessly unimaginative imitation preachers repeat the dull pattern of calling it the "parable of the prodigal son." But what could be better devised to destroy the point of it than that label? Actually in the parable no such term as "prodigal" occurs; the power of the parable is in facts, not adjectives. The lad who is its central character is not to be separated from a host of other maturing boys by being tagged with a bad name. When the essentially decent boys and young men in a congregation hear the preacher announce that he is preaching on "the prodigal son," they settle back with a cool detachment that recognizes no direct relationship of this exordium to them. Let the preacher go on, if he wants to, with this moralistic obviousness that has indicated his conclusion in advance; it does not get hold of them. But the real parable does get hold of them. For it is the inescapable story of a younger generation that is always being born—the story of the nearly grown boy who has no deliberate badness in him, but is just impatient and cocksure. He thinks he has had enough of controls. He wants "to see life for himself, to go out on his own." He is smart enough, he thinks, to make his own way and to have a much better time doing it. But the clinching fact is that things do not work out that way. Without any original intention, but just because of his recklessness and ignorance, he is snared by vicious influences. Then he comes to himself—the self that knows it belongs at home and not in the alien country. And by identification with that kind of boy, and not through a lecture on "the prodigal," the boys in a congregation may get the message that this parable holds for them.

Or consider another great New Testament passage. The parable of the good Samaritan is so swift and sure that no one can miss its central truth. Yet it may be questioned whether most sermons bring home the absolute finality of Jesus' answer, cutting through the lawyer's question with the sharpness of the sword. This man who was like so many who think they would like to be good if it can be made not too inconvenient asked Jesus, "Who is my neighbor?" He wanted Jesus to draw a circle that would let his duty be defined. "Who is your neighbor? Your family, your kinsfolk, the people with whom you have natural associations. Those who have been good to you, so that you ought to be good to them." That was the sort of answer the lawyer wanted. If the circle of definition could be drawn precisely enough, perhaps he could manage to be kind to all the "neighbors" included in it; and then by natural inference he would be free from bothering about the people outside. But Jesus set the whole matter in a completely different light. He told the story of a man who needed

119

a "neighbor," and of the three men who in the presence of that need revealed what sort of persons they were: "Which of these three, do you think, proved neighbor to the man who fell among the robbers?" The lawyer had to admit that it was the one who showed mercy on him. So his own little question of "Who is my neighbor?" went unanswered, and instead he got the challenge of determining how many he was willing to be neighbor to. It was as though Jesus said, "To be kind, and to be a neighbor, is no grudging obligation; it is an opportunity, and the question is as to whether you are man enough to seize it."

Or turn to a more important instance. One may hear in the course of years many sermons on the temptations of Jesus, and for some reason—is it only because of the accident that when the preacher opens his New Testament, he comes upon this Gospel first?—nearly all of them are based on the account in the Gospel of Matthew. In Matthew's account the temptation listed second is that of the devil's suggestion that Jesus go and throw himself down from a pinnacle of the Temple and be unhurt. Again and again this temptation is preached about as though it were a subordinate one sandwiched in between the two others, and as though its meaning is that Jesus considered giving a miraculous exhibition that would leave all the people astonished at his power. But such an idea is thin and poor in comparison with the thought that can wake as one goes forward to read the account in the Gospel of Luke. There this temptation is put as the last and therefore the climactic one—and how deep is the spiritual reality embodied there! Here in truth was the most profound and awful test of Jesus' dedication. He had already rejected the temptation to seek the people's favor by ministering to the immediate wants of those who would follow him for the

120

loaves and fishes, and the temptation to be the kind of conquering Messiah, using this world's weapon to win a world dominion, which the Zealots wanted. Now it was as though the tempter bade him claim reward for all that consecration. Let him expect that God henceforth would surround him with unmistakable blessing and protection. No matter what danger he might now face, no matter if it were as extreme as falling from a pinnacle of the Temple, God's angels would protect him from any hurt. It was only *right* that he should expect that, said the tempter; therefore expect it. Go on in God's way if God would do his part; take up God's work, *provided*. This was indeed the ultimate temptation, and conquest over it represented the ultimate heroism of accepting the possibility of disaster and of a foreshadowed cross. How close that temptation brings Jesus to that which can be the most terrible testing of our own faith—to the dark moments when a life that has tried to be devoted to God must keep its trust even when not happiness but pain and suffering bring what seems their contradiction.

All those are illustrations of the truth that John Robinson expressed in his farewell sermon to the Pilgrims, "There is yet more truth to break forth out of God's Holy Word." And if those illustrations do not kindle the thought of a particular man, there are plenty of others in the New Testament which he can make his own.

In the New Testament, as in the Old, there is inspiration for sermons in the human figures who followed Jesus and played their parts in the early Church.

First, there are the Twelve—the group within which were men so varied and some of them of strengths and weaknesses so familiar that every man in his experience may feel at some

121

point akin to them. The big fisherman from Galilee to whom Jesus said when he first saw him, "So you are Simon the son of John?" and then went on to the promise that should turn this warmhearted but unstable man into the great person that his Master's confidence would make him be, "You shall be called Cephas (which means [Rock])" (John 1:42); Andrew, the man of quiet faithfulness who was not soured when his brother overshadowed him; James and John, the "sons of thunder," one of whom should become regarded as above all others the disciple who most knew Jesus' love; Thomas, with his mind that doubted but his loyalty that would not let go; Matthew, who left his tax collector's profit for the stronger pull that Jesus had upon his soul; others of that Twelve, the men of whom nothing conspicuous is known and who by that very fact of their seeming unimportance give to every humble Christian the dignity of knowing that a life like his can count in the eyes of Jesus—such are some of the figures in the Gospels whom the preacher can make live again within his people's recognition.

One of the particular ways in which a man can help his congregation is by preaching now and then a series of sermons on a continuous theme. The possibilities of this with the figures of the New Testament are plain to see. As there could be a series on some of the Twelve, so likewise there could be a series on Paul. Instead of merely an occasional reference to something that he said, a congregation might thus get some systematic and reasonably adequate conception of the personality of that great apostle and of his imperishable contribution to Christian life and thought. Similarly there might be a series on those friends of his without whom his own full work would have been impossible and whose lives are witness to what can always be the greatness in God's service of the

122

so-called lesser men: Barnabas, the "good man, full of the Holy Spirit," whose name was given to him by the disciples for the heart-warming reason that he seemed to them a "Son of encouragement"; Luke, the beloved physician; Silas; Timothy; Epaphras; Titus; and the blessed, indispensable, but not even named people who made up the sustaining Christian fellowship, such as the one of whom there is only a lovely hint when in the last chapter of the letter to the Romans, Paul sends his greetings not only to Rufus but also to "his mother and mine."

A series of sermons on another note could be preached on those men in the New Testament who either in deliberate evil rejected what might have been their great God-given opportunity, or by the tragic error of too little and too late let that opportunity slip by: Judas; Caiaphas; Herod; Pilate; Nicodemus; Joseph of Arimathea, a "disciple of Jesus, but secretly," whose only recorded evidence of loyalty was the offer of a grave for the crucified Jesus to be buried in.

The value of a series that develops particular sermons within the bond of one embracing interest should be clear. It gives the congregation something to think of on one Sunday that will be more surely remembered because it is linked in interest with what they listened to the Sunday before and can expect on the Sunday after. It increases their respect for the minister because they can see that his preaching is not a hasty hand-to-mouth affair, but is the fruit of genuine forethought and preparation on their behalf. And for exactly that reason the preaching of a sermon series is wholesome discipline for the man himself. When he has committed himself to develop a large theme, he will have a solidity of purpose and an expanding interest that does not belong to the man who scratches up some accidental subject from the thin straw of Saturday-night ideas.

Besides those which have been suggested, there are in the New Testament veins for preaching so rich and so wide that a man need never be at a loss to know where he may dig gold. There are the inexhaustible parables of Jesus, the Beatitudes, and the rest of the Sermon on the Mount; the story of the early Church in the book of Acts; the special message in each of the epistles. Henry Sloane Coffin in the first chapter of his *What to Preach* reminds his fellow preachers that "there is a wealthy course of sermons in the questions put to Jesus . . . an even more heart-searching course in the questions put by Jesus," and another course in the questions asked concerning Jesus. And in his *Communion Through Preaching* he gives a luminous example of an expository sermon at its best—luminous as to both the content and the form which must belong to expository preaching when it is great. No sort of preaching can be more misunderstood and more poorly done than this. Properly it is the direct elucidation and interpretation of a particular part of scripture, most characteristically of a lengthy part; and the trouble with many preachers is that when thus confronted with a wide area of the scripture, they become bewildered and cannot see it as a whole. So what they do is to make a few groping comments on each successive verse, like a blind man tapping his way with a stick. But in order to guide the thought of a congregation effectively, the scripture must be seen in its full perspective and in the entirety of meaning within which the several elements find their sure relationship. It is not a mechanical matter of stating one detail after another; it is a creative grasp of what the whole passage says and a setting forth of this with such selection, abridgment, or rearrangement of the details as will

124

make the great pattern unmistakable. And this is what Dr. Coffin does when he suggests a sermon on the whole book of Revelation—a sermon which brings the message of that flaming book directly into touch with troubled modern times. "It can be done," he writes, "under four heads."

And these four—followed in his pages by an expansion of their meaning—are these:

1. The certain downfall of the dominant secular culture.
2. The continuing instability to be expected when a great culture breaks up.
3. The Church, through which God carries out His main purpose in history, is represented in Chapters two and three by seven flickering lamps showing against the black darkness of a doomed world.
4. The climax of history is the arrival of the city of God.

That book of Revelation which stands at the end of the New Testament brings to its climax a note that runs through the whole New Testament like the tolling of a solemn bell. It is the recognition that an era in human history was drawing to its close. Not only would Jerusalem be destroyed; not only would the vast structure of Roman rule be broken and the life of its wide provinces pass into a long eclipse of darkness and disorder. In and beyond these portentous events the early Christians saw the tokens of a cataclysm which they believed would be universal and complete. Under God's judgment the present world and its wickedness must disappear, and only in a new kingdom of the redeemed could life go on. What happened did not follow in outward aspects the particular picture which the early Christians had in mind—the picture of fire from heaven destroying this physical earth and the inauguration of Christ's kingdom in visible glory. Nevertheless the essential facts which they foresaw came true. Human life in what had been the Roman Empire descended into its dark ages, and only the little companies of Christians kept the light of hope and purpose burning. Out of this New Testament background comes a message which has poignant and immediate meaning for another century of disruption. The minds of contemporary men and women are full of the realization that they too are living at the end of an era. The development of atomic weapons and the whole ominous threat of the global conflict have made them acutely conscious of a possible catastrophe as dreadful as that which the first century conceived. Great Christian preaching must have a profundity which matches that awareness. It must have an equal emphasis upon a world-wide Christian fellowship which alone can be the saving element through whatever shocks may fall upon the human race. It must be a voice not of defeatism, but of courage—a voice that will call individuals and nations to the dedicated purpose and decisions which may be saving if they are not too late. The sort of preaching which will lay hold of men's minds and wills must have the New Testament's urgency and the thrust of New Testament language which can be so much more plain and powerful than that of some New Testament commentators. It will not talk about the "eschatological aspect of history," nor use any other six-syllable adjective. It will make people face the instant need of works fit for repentance, lest the moment come when all that can be said will be, "The door was shut."

Such, then, are some of the multidinous texts and themes in the New Testament from which a man can preach. But the supreme message is over and above all these. It enters into each one of them and gives to each one its measure of inspiration. In the words of the great Apostle we preach "Jesus Christ, and him crucified," who "being raised from the dead dieth no more; death hath no more dominion over him. For in that he died, he died unto sin once: but in that he liveth, he liveth unto God. Likewise reckon ye also yourselves to be dead indeed unto sin, but alive unto God through Jesus Christ our Lord!" (Rom. 6:9-11.)

That is the burning and shining truth which is at the center of Christian proclamation and from which every particular sermon must draw its light. That is the evangel. It includes convictions which are as indivisible and yet as infinitely outreaching as a flame.

In the first place here was the supreme Event. In the life of Jesus, in his crucifixion, in his rising again, in his return to his disciples, something happened in the midst of history, because of which all history before that Event and all history after it are transfigured. In Jesus Christ the long hopes and yearning of the Old Testament have their fulfillment, and in him the faith and purpose of men for all the years to come find their meaning and direction. The fact that for most of the nations of the world the calendar is reckoned from the birth of Jesus Christ, with the years preceding him listed as "before Christ" and those following him as "anno Domini," is a perpetual symbol of human awareness of the crucial effect of his entrance into human history. Even when men do not think explicitly about it, they bear thus their silent witness to the supreme importance of his appearing.

And when thought does dwell deeply upon it, it grows plain that here the fundamental realities of human life and destiny converge—good and evil, light and darkness, God's purpose and man's resistance, and God's supremacy at the last. In the great figures of the Old Testament one gets glimpses of what character can be: the faithfulness of Abraham, the moral stamina and the magnanimity of Joseph, the heroic dedication of Moses, the fearlessness of Elijah, the compassion of Hosea. Looking at Jesus, one sees all those elements of partial goodness included and transcended in the life of which the judgment of mankind has had to say with reverence what Pilate said indifferently, "I find no fault in him." But against this the other aspect of the human spirit is brought to its corresponding focus. There is the awful fact that the very perfection of Jesus made the opposition of many men all the more implacable. They resisted him not only because they did not understand him, but because in one sense they understood him only too well. When a certain small boy dropped out of Sunday school, the teacher asked his sister what had become of him; and this was the startling answer: "Well, to tell you the truth, he just can't stand Jesus." That idea came out of the small boy's ignorance and twisted misunderstanding: out of the impression he had got from Sunday-school chromos of Jesus done in heliotrope and pink and baby blue, a Jesus who seemed to him feeble and inconsequential, a Jesus who bored him because he thought that kind of Jesus did not matter. But grown men who knew the real Jesus could not stand him either, and not because of ignorance but because of knowledge. They saw in him a power they did not want to have to reckon with. His purity rebuked their secret lust; his moral demands rebuked their compromises; his immense compassion for all human souls rebuked their prejudices; his call to the kingdom of God threatened their profitable engrossment with the kingdoms of this world. He made them too uncomfortable. And since they could not get rid of him in any other way, they reached the point where they were ready to have him crucified—those men whose characteristic, as

128

Archbishop Temple once said, was not that they were notoriously wicked, but rather that they were as good as we are and no better.

Thus appears the everlasting significance of Jesus Christ and him crucified. When the light of God comes into the midst of human affairs, the darkness that is in men's wills wants to put it out. Conscience recognizes it, but the unregenerate self repudiates it. Not only was that true in the first century; it may be true in every century. That is the way a part of human nature is, and that is the way it recurrently responds. In every man there may be something of the Herod spirit that does not want the heavenly king to come into its world and endanger its own control, something of the Caiaphas spirit that hates the new and challenging, something of the cowardice of Peter that can deny even what it loves, something of the treachery of Judas that will sell the Christ who has not measured up to its selfish expectations.

Seen thus, the whole event of Jesus' life and crucifixion becomes the theme of the Christian preacher's deepest meditation. Out of the fact of it, so glorious and so awful, comes the kind of preaching that is most passionate and most redeeming—as of a John Wesley, a Dwight L. Moody, a Studdert-Kennedy. It is no detached recital of an ancient story. It is the confrontation of living men with the eternal tragedy that may be repeated in them: the wonder of God rebuffed by human wickedness, the love of God crucified by human sin. When the man who is to preach sees that and feels that, then into his preaching can come an utter personal humility and yet a limitless representative power, because he knows that he is the ambassador of the message that transcends himself—the message that mingles contrition and hope, an awful moral urgency and a divine compassion, the flame of judgment and the healing touch of the love of God.

In the mid-twentieth century what is sometimes the more somber note in the Christian proclamation has tended to be predominant. There is a new realization—or rather a very old realization now again grown conscious—of the power of the evil that actually exists in individuals and in society. When one looks at the horrible things that have been part of twentieth-century history—the fanatical nationalistic and race hatreds, the organized brutalities, the indiscriminate destruction—it seems not exaggerated to call such a record demonic. In the face of it there is no room for the bland and easy self-confidence, too often settling down into a complacent humanism, which had begun to appear in the early 1900's. Two world wars and the dark forces of the jungle which they let loose put an end to the shallow incantation that "day by day in every way we are growing better and better." It may seem instead that, left to our own devices, moment by moment we grow worse and worse. Consequently, as men have read the New Testament, they have done so with a new perception. They turn to the letters of Paul and to his relentless emphasis upon the profundity of human sin, and there is a wide echo of his cry, "O wretched man that I am! who shall deliver me from the body of this death?" (Rom. 7:24).

This present humbling of self-sufficiency is a wholesome thing. When the human spirit is stripped of its false pride, it is at the point where it begins to know that only something much bigger and better than itself can be saving. So it is ready to listen to the Pauline gospel of a grace that comes from God alone. It stands in reverence before what may be to its understanding the "mystery, which from the beginning of the world hath been hid in God," but which, to him who is

130

grasped by it, can bring the "unsearchable riches of Christ."
Men today may be drawn toward the great conviction which
flamed in Martin Luther's words, "Lo, to me, an unworthy,
condemned, and contemptible creature, altogether without
merit, my God of His pure and free mercy has given in Christ
all the riches of righteousness and salvation, so that I am no
longer in want of anything except faith to believe this is so."

Preaching from the New Testament, especially where the
influence of Karl Barth and the neo-orthodox movement is
strong, has concentrated anew upon this faith. It proclaims
the ultimate act of the grace of God which achieves for men
imprisoned in their insufficiency and sin a deliverance which
no human merit could deserve or achieve. It is the message
that comes to those who again "survey the wondrous cross."
Christ crucified, Christ risen, Christ as Lord in the kingdom
of the Spirit—this is the reaffirmation of the gospel that Paul
preached. It swings directly away from the idea which sometimes has been smoothly advanced—that we need to know
the "religion of Jesus and stop formulating so much religion
about Jesus." There have been periods when that idea was
popular and when it was supposed that Christianity in order
to be intelligent must say only what is obvious and generally
acceptable. Thomas Jefferson took the Gospels and abbreviated
them into what he called the "Morals of Jesus." It was doubt-
less his sincere belief that it was a service to Christianity to
eliminate what seemed to him the supernatural and thus to
commend Christianity to rationalists. Other individuals and
church groups in varying degree have let their thoughts move
in the same direction. Jesus—they have held—was the great
teacher and exemplar of morals, a man superlatively good.
What better could be said than that? Learn of him, imitate

131

him, and you also can be good. So a man can attain to character which is its own salvation.

But the trouble with this is that it does not work. It rates human capability too high, and it fails to see the transcendent meaning not only of what Jesus taught but of what he was. The chastening fact is that men cannot just listen to his teaching and then smoothly make up their minds to obey it and thus be good, as he was good. The gap between what they are and what he represented is too wide for any moral effort of their own to bridge. If they presume to think otherwise, the result—as the great Apostle knew—is disillusionment and near despair. Deliverance comes only when the great truth dawns—the truth that God has done what humanity by itself could never do. His mercy has reached down to those who could not reach up to him. In Jesus, living, dying, and alive again, something unique has happened. Remembering that matchless life that accepted its rejection by the sins of men, and standing before the cross that is the witness to the utter length to which the redeeming love of God will go, men and women in every time have known what John Wesley knew that night when the wonder of the gospel came to him in the chapel in Aldersgate Street and made him say: "I felt my heart strangely warmed. I felt I did trust in Christ, Christ alone for salvation; and an assurance was given me that He had taken away my sins, even *mine*, and saved me from the law of sin and death." [4] Souls that could never explain the doctrine of the Atonement have thus experienced it. They have found new life in Christ. So it is right that men who preach should give the New Testament message in its divine fullness. It must not be cut and trimmed to suit the casual understanding. Its meaning has the dimensions of infinity, which lie beyond the

[4] *Wesley's Journal*, May 24, 1728.

grasp of that complacent wisdom of this world which by comparison is only foolishness.

But another and co-ordinate emphasis is needed in Christian preaching. Jesus Christ and him crucified—that is the substance of the gospel. The last four words of those five represent the culminating truth: the mystery of the Cross and the power of the New Being that arises from it. But there is a risk that this may become abstract. The Cross, the Christ, the New Being—yes, but who was the Christ, and what is the nature of the New Being? To answer those questions, one must go back of the Pauline theology to the Gospels and try directly to apprehend Jesus. Jesus as the first disciples knew him; Jesus with his friends and his foes; Jesus facing the dramatic choices and making the fateful decisions that turned his road toward Jerusalem and Calvary; Jesus with his overwhelming authority in the midst of the human scene; Jesus who died, but first had so greatly lived—preach *him*, and the Christian evangel has the fire of devotion which always has carried it most movingly into the hearts of men.

Unless this Jesus of the whole gospel story grows clear, the body and substance would disappear from the throbbing Christian conviction of a Redeemer made incarnate. Not any Christ-idea, not some unspecified New Being, not even the most majestic framework of speculative thought, can answer the needs of human beings who want someone to take hold of and to take hold of them. What is it that makes the gospel of Jesus Christ not just a wistful imagination concerning a Saviour-God? It is the fact that the Christ of Pauline and all later theology was the actual *Master* to whom Paul, like the earlier disciples, gave his life: no mystical construct, but the actual figure who had walked this earth, of whom those who

133

first followed him could say, "We have heard, . . . we have seen with our eyes, . . . have looked upon, and our hands have handled" (I John 1:1), and because of the sort of life he actually lived, and because he touched their lives and gave them illimitable meaning, they saw for the first time concretely what God in the midst of humanity could be. It was this actuality, this particularity of quality and of spirit that shone in *him*, which gave substance to both the tragedy and the glory of the crucified and risen Lord. Belief in a man crucified and a man risen would have meant no more than another mystery tale. The incomparable tragedy was that it was Jesus, *this* man with his purity, his unflinching courage and devotion, his love so outreaching that men could think of it in no less measurement than the measure of what must be the love of God—it was *this* one who revealed in the world's crucifixion of him the dreadful possibilities of human sin, and it was *this* one whose resurrection was credible because only in the ultimate triumph of a life like his could the whole scheme of things make sense.

Yet the man who is to preach today may say, "Ah, but how can I really know Jesus?" He lived so long ago, and how can we come close to him again?

> Dim tracts of time divide
> Those golden days from me.[5]

So it may seem. And this sense of Jesus as remote may become greater and more oppressive when one listens to some of the theories of New Testament form criticism. All that we have, so such theories suggest, are fragments of tradition, seen through the perspective of later faith. The actual historic Jesus we cannot recapture. Floyd V. Filson writes:

[5] Francis T. Palgrave, "Thou say'st, take up thy cross."

Ostensibly a pure historical discipline [form criticism] often operates with philosophical and theological presuppositions which derive tradition from process rather than from a great creative figure. Hence form criticism has occasionally led to a practical agnosticism as to what Jesus said and did. To be sure, it is a valuable corrective to the purely literary study which divorced the writings of the Gospels from the life of the Church. It has shown how the tradition was used in the worship, teaching and controversy of the first Christians. But at times it has almost reduced Jesus to an unknown X.[6]

But the everlasting wonder is that the Jesus whom some think we cannot recapture nevertheless recaptures us. Through all the fog of learned reasons why we cannot find him, he finds us. However or whenever the pages of the Gospels were composed, the immense reality of Jesus emerges from them. Not only to the great seers and saints, such as Bernard of Clairvaux, but to the lowliest men and women who have humbly read the Gospels, he has come, as the "Joy of loving hearts," the "Fount of life," the "Light of men." Let every man who is to go into a Christian pulpit know that and proclaim it! Let him preach Christ whose meaning and significance we may know best when we are simplest, as when in the poignant intuition of the Negro spiritual we sing:

> Lord, I want to be like Jesus
> In my heart.

When a man does start his thought with what he feels in Jesus, as Jesus actually comes to him out of the pages of the Gospels, there will still be questions he cannot answer; but he will have the vital conviction that he is in touch, and can bring his people into touch, with the way, the truth, and the

[6] *Protestant Thought in the Twentieth Century*, Arnold S. Nash, ed. (New York: The Macmillan Co., 1951), p. 55.

life. A meaning in existence begins to emerge. Life, with its sunlight and its shadow, its glories and its tragedies, its Galilees and its Gethsemanes, does have something warm to trust in and to live for, because there has been Jesus and because the deathless power of God in him has been let loose in our world.

SUGGESTIONS FOR SUPPLEMENTARY READING

Brown, William Adams. *How to Think of Christ*. New York: Chas. Scribner's Sons, 1945.

Dodd, C. H. *The Apostolic Preaching*. New York: Harper & Bros., 1950.

——. *Gospel and Law*. New York: Columbia University Press, 1951.

The Interpreter's Bible. New York and Nashville: Abingdon Press. Vols. VII-XII.

Nygren, Anders. *The Gospel of God*. Tr. L. J. Trinterud. Philadelphia: Westminster Press, 1951.

Stewart, James S. *A Man in Christ*. New York: Harper & Bros., 1935.

CHAPTER EIGHT

Relating Theology to Life

A MAN'S CREED does not matter; it is what he does that counts." This is a notion often expressed that is as false as it is shallow. A man's creed, in the deep sense of what he fundamentally believes in and wants to be loyal to, will determine what the man will do. It has been trenchantly said that it is more important for a landlady to know whether her tenant believes in honesty than to know how much money he has. If he does believe in honesty, he will somehow get the money to pay her; and if he does not, he may abscond, no matter how much money he happens to have.

Every man has a creed, whether or not he says it out loud. He may believe in rascality or in righteousness, in devices for his own gain or in the sense of duty that comes to him from God. His theology, or lack of it, is not separable from his character and life. That is why it is foolish to suppose, as some churchgoers and even some ministers do, that theological preaching is not practical preaching. It is as practical as laying the foundation for a house. As the Sermon on the Mount reminds us, the house of character that is not built upon the rock of the accepted truth of God is a weak thing that will collapse when the time of testing comes.

So there is no either-or choice between what is called "life-

137

situation preaching" and the preaching of theology. Every sermon ought to be related to the needs of life, but those needs cannot be taken care of by second-story carpentering; they must be undergirded by convictions that go deep down. "Can my life have any fundamental certainties? Can I rely not on my own manufactured props, but on a reality of God so sure that it cannot be shaken?" Those are the decisive questions which a man wants answered. It will not be enough to give him smooth prescriptions as to how to deal with his anxieties, how to integrate his personality, how to make friends and be successful, if he thinks the universe he lives in is just an ugly mechanism where the cards are stacked against him anyway. The human being is capable of high purpose and steady courage, but only as long as he believes that the whole business of living makes sense; and in order to keep on thinking that it does make sense, he reaches out in search of an ultimate meaning, good and great, into which his life can find its place.

Here is where theology comes in.

The *Book of Common Prayer*, with reference to the Christian creed, asks the question: "What dost thou chiefly learn in these Articles of thy Belief?" And the first answer is that we believe in God who is our Father and that it is this God the Father who has made us and all the world.

Obviously it does not always seem so. Life is confronted with contradictions and perplexities. There are hurts and disappointments. There are roads we try to walk on, only to be brought up short before some mystery we cannot fathom. There is evil; there are moments when the best we know seems beaten; there is the tragic fact of death. Can all this mean that goodness is at the heart of things? No, says the voice

138

of doubt. But the Christian faith says yes! And the shining commission of the Christian preacher is to proclaim that faith. He will not pretend to have an answer to all questions. He will not foolishly suppose, or let his congregation suppose, that our finite minds are expected to see all the way into the infinite. But neither will he just hand out dogmatic statements that have no evidence in life. He will tell men that trust in God is a venture of faith, but a venture that justifies the impulse of the heart that makes it. All the good and gallant lives of Christian history, all the agelong witness of the Christian fellowship, fortify his message that there is a power of experience which overthrows the pessimism of the doubting mind. Those who go out into the world daring to believe that goodness has made it and that in the act of living they will find life good have found it so—found it so not in ease and shallow happiness, but in the great expansion of souls that have come into touch with God and so have begun to grow. This is an approach to theology which ordinary people can understand because they can try it. To let one's life venture upon the goodness of God is like launching a boat from the still, shallow water by the bank out into the river where it finds the strong current that runs to the sea.

The second supreme article of faith is summed up as belief "in God the Son, who hath redeemed me, and all mankind." Brief words, but in them, as into clear, still water, we look down into depths beyond our fathoming. The uniqueness of Christianity is in the conviction that in Jesus Christ, God, the infinite and invisible, "has spoken to us by a Son," who "reflects the glory of God and bears the very stamp of his nature" (Heb. 1:2-3 R.S.V.). Every religion has worshiped some sort of God. But what sort? Sometimes men's conception of the one to whom they bow down has been shaped from

139

clouded emotions of groping wonder and awe and dread as they met the forces of the physical universe: the brightness of spring and the darkness of winter, the shining of the sun and the terror of an eclipse, thunder and lightning, earthquake and volcanic fire. Sometimes their conception of God has been shaped from speculative thought and sometimes from mystical and poetic intuitions that could rise to great nobility. But the Christian faith both goes beyond these and comes nearer. It is the faith that for the souls of men the eternal God has revealed himself in a life lived in their midst and through which they could understand and be touched by the Divine. Here is the eternal answer to the wistful search of human hearts for a near and saving God.

> So, the All-Great, were the All-Loving too—
> So, through the thunder comes a human voice
> Saying, "O heart I made, a heart beats here." [1]

And through Jesus, thus God and man, living, dying, and now forever alive, we are redeemed: redeemed from bewilderment, from lostness, from the burden of sins that would be intolerable if they were unforgiven. Here is the realm, then, in which Christian preaching moves. It can include all the immensities of thought to which Paul and all great theologians have shown the way, but at the center of it is the Jesus of the Gospels, whose appeal to them even the simplest and humblest know.

The third article of the faith, as it stands in the ancient words of the Apostles' Creed, begins, "I believe in the Holy Ghost"—or as it would be in the words of our more familiar speech, "I believe in the Holy Spirit." Here again is em-

[1] Robert Browning, "An Epistle."

bodied the fact that theology and the right kind of theological preaching are no abstractions, but have to do with what is incomparably warm and vital and immediate. For belief in the Holy Spirit means that God's manifestation of himself is not far off either in place or in time. We do not have to think of him as only in the awful immensities of the universe, nor as come near to us once, but only once, and that in the life that is dated nineteen hundred years ago. The Holy Spirit is the continuing operation of the grace and power that were seen in Jesus. The little impulses toward goodness in Christian people, which might seem so inadequate and weak if they were only their own, are *not* only their own—not the mere bubbles of their own desires, but the welling up in them of the Holy Spirit. And it is because of this Spirit that we can believe in the Church not as a voluntary club of self-sufficient individuals, but in its ideal as Paul saw it to be—the body of Christ, the extension of the Incarnation in which the Spirit dwells. And it is because of this same Spirit that we can dare proclaim "the communion of saints, the forgiveness of sins, the resurrection of the body, and the life everlasting."

Let no man in a Christian pulpit forget that the people there before him hunger to lay hold now upon those convictions which the ancient words affirm. What happened to be disclosed in one particular church and in the year 1953 is significant of many churches and of a time that reaches—as life does—far beyond a special date. A number of young parents, more than a hundred, were asked to choose among twenty-four subjects the ones they thought most vital for them to consider and to try to understand; and the two that stood decisively as their first and second choices were these: "Some trends in modern theological thinking" and "What is the Christian interpretation of death?" In a world that is full of

141

uncertainty and menace men and women are reaching out for answers to those questions which touch them at the level of their deepest needs. So they want theology—a knowledge of God and an assurance from God that will help them to believe that in him there is a communion of all saintly lives, the living and the dead, by which they may be strengthened; a forgiveness of sins through the cleansing mercy that does not depend upon their own deserving; and a life beyond this present life in which God will bring to fulfillment the best that we have begun to learn here.

Men who are to preach the gospel should hold often in their own meditations, and then communicate to their people, the fact that all great and true theology commenced in life. It has not been the product of theoretical thinkers sitting down somewhere to evolve their speculations. It has been the effort to put into transmissible terms what men have been possessed by in their spiritual experience. Always the forms of expression have been less than adequate, and sometimes they have come to seem as formulas so frozen in antique language that ordinary Christians cannot draw the meaning from them. The business of the preacher is to bring them back from the abstract into the living and relevant reality where they began. Take, for example, that seemingly most difficult doctrine—the doctrine of the Trinity. In the historic prayer for Trinity Sunday the congregation thanks God that he has given to us "grace, by the confession of a true faith, to acknowledge the glory of the eternal Trinity, and in the power of the Divine Majesty to worship the Unity." It is safe to say that most Christian worshipers will listen to those words with only a pious acquiescence; as to what they mean they probably have not the dimmest actual notion. And this not only for the reason that the infinite wonder of God will

142

in any case transcend our utmost thought, but for the further reason that in those abstruse words they cannot yet find the key to the meaning which the Trinity does have for their living minds and hearts.

To find the key, one must go back of the speculative phrases to the experiences in life from which they came. The doctrine of the Trinity by name is nowhere in the New Testament, but the beginnings of it are there. They appear in the beautiful and familiar benediction of the apostle Paul, "The grace of the Lord Jesus Christ and the love of God, and the fellowship of the Holy Spirit be with you all" (II Cor. 13:14 R.S.V.).

There the order of remembrance is different from the order of the three great affirmations in the Apostles' Creed. The creed has systematized that which Christians had learned to believe, and so it is faith in God the Creator and Father that is proclaimed first. But the benediction reflects the actual sequence of experience in which the awarenesses that are unique in Christianity dawned. They began with the "grace of the Lord Jesus Christ."

Because they were Jews and inheritors of the Old Testament, the first disciples already knew and worshiped God. But their whole conception of God and of their relationship to God was set in a new light when they came into touch with Jesus. The Twelve had lived with Jesus, and they had felt the authority of his words and of his life. They saw in him a spirit that simply was not of the earth they had known before. By his courage he gave them courage. Because of his confidence in them they began to have confidence in what God could make of them. By his understanding and compassion he helped them to feel, even when they were most ashamed of their weaknesses, that he saw something better

143

in them and that by his love they might begin to measure up to his expectations. That was the grace of the Lord Jesus. And after the Resurrection the disciples were sure that this grace of their Lord was still with them. The risen Christ in whose power they went out to preach was the risen Jesus. Therefore God—the God whose name had been on their lips in the ancient prayers of Israel, the God whose law they had listened to as they heard the scriptures in the synagogue, the God whose presence they had sought on the great holy days in the Temple—had a warmer meaning for their hearts as they thought of him as the Father of the Master they had known and loved.

But what of Paul himself, who wrote of the "grace of the Lord Jesus Christ"? There are those who hold that Paul had no direct knowledge of Jesus and little concern with his earthly life. He was absorbed—so it is argued—in the one supreme fact of a sacrificial death upon the cross for the sins of men, the mystical identification of sinful men in the death of the Redeemer, and their spiritual rising again with him in his resurrection. There is immense and moving truth in that conviction concerning the Atonement and the new life in the risen Christ—a conviction that lifts Christian faith up to the mighty level of a salvation dependent not upon men's little efforts, but upon the one vast fact of the forgiveness of God revealed upon the cross. But if there is not equal emphasis upon who it was that died upon the cross, then what the great Apostle really believed and lived by can be reduced—as some so-called Pauline theologians have reduced it—to one more mystery drama of an etherealized dying and rising Saviour-God. Paul's faith was no such speculative fog. It is only a shallow conception of him and of his whole life that

144

does not feel his throbbing devotion to the immediate reality of Jesus.

Had he ever seen Jesus in the flesh? "It is no unsupported phantasy," wrote W. M. Macgregor, "that Paul, though with jaundiced eyes, had seen Jesus, thinking of Him only as a disturber of the worship of God, and that the memory of the encounter had remained with him, like a fragrance, subtly influencing thought and memory and feeling."

But what if Paul, when he was Saul of Tarsus, had not thus seen Jesus? Would this mean that he had not come in a deep sense to know him? Consider the facts. As a Pharisee in Jerusalem he could not have helped hearing about Jesus. What he heard would of course have been distorted by the hostility through which it came, but not the less on that account would he have had a powerful impression of the challenging importance of this man of Nazareth. Then came the martyrdom of Stephen, with Saul of Tarsus standing by, and afterward the invincible memory of the look on Stephen's face and the sound of his dying voice as he prayed, "Lord Jesus, receive my spirit." In Jerusalem, Saul must have heard of Peter's preaching, even if one chooses to assume that he did not hear it with his own ears. Then what happened? Saul went out with fanatical determination to hunt down Christians wherever he could find them. In the way they bore themselves and in their confessions he was meeting the same reality of Jesus which he had seen—and tried not to see—in Stephen. What made him keep on as a persecutor? A sure conviction that he was right? Or a desperate effort to suppress the new awareness of what Jesus was like, which woke in him a response that grew more and more irresistible? It is this latter assumption that explains the terrific impact of his conversion vision. How did he know that the light

145

he saw and the voice he heard on the road to Damascus was *Jesus* except that the picture of Jesus had been building up in his unwilling mind and heart? And after his conversion, when he went out to preach the glory of the risen Christ, can anyone miss the personal devotion to Jesus his Master which rings through all that he preached and wrote? "I count everything as loss because of the surpassing worth of knowing Christ Jesus my Lord." (Phil. 3:8 R.S.V.)

As James Stewart has written in that rich book *A Man in Christ*:

No doubt there have been Christians who have sat loose to history; but Paul was not one of them. He had the genius to see that in a world full of fantasies and myths and cults and mysteries, it was precisely in its historic basis that the new religion's strength and promise of victory lay. . . . To say that history meant little or nothing to Paul is simply not true: it meant everything to him. As Denney put it: "Paul could not in his work as an evangelist preach salvation through the death and resurrection of an unknown person; the story which was the common property of the Church, and with which her catechists everywhere indoctrinated the new disciples, must have been as familiar to him, in substance, as it is to us." As familiar? Far more so. Sayings of our Lord and incidents of His life now unknown to us may well have been in the knowledge of His great apostle. The earthly and heavenly Christ were one; and never while Paul gloried in his daily fellowship with the eternally living Redeemer did he cease to ponder on the life and walk and character of One who by entering history had changed all history forever.[2]

Let every Christian preacher therefore ponder as deeply as he can the mighty interpretations which Paul gave to the dying, rising, and atoning Christ; but let him never forget that at the heart of it all is the Jesus, near and real and understand-

[2] Pp. 285-86. Used by permission of Harper & Bros.

able, who comes to us continually anew from the pages of the Gospels to make us know what manner of life it is into which we are to be redeemed. It is not by the interpretation of even the greatest of the apostles, but by the direct impact of their Lord Jesus, that we are saved.

It has been memorably said, by Henry Sloane Coffin, that the doctrine of the Deity of Jesus Christ is not so much a doctrine about Jesus as it is a doctrine about God. We are not left to speculations about the invisible; we can remember that which was made visible and understand and know what was forever reflected there. Christian faith is not dependent upon arguments from ontology and cosmology and teleology and other speculations which may seem remote. The center of its trust is in what comes close to every mind and heart. It is in the conviction that in Jesus, as he lived and died, we see the very nature of God. Jesus is the focal point from which all our conceptions of God begin. To accept him as the ultimate revelation means that as we project our thought into the infinite, we shall find nothing there which is inconsistent with what we have seen in Jesus. God the Creator and Sustainer, God who is the beginning and end of all our life, is the One whom we have beheld in the Incarnation. That is the truth, the supreme and essential truth, which was struggling for expression in what impatiently and mistakenly might be supposed to be only a controversy about words in the Nicene Creed, as between *homoiousia* and *homoousia*. Athanasius and those who followed him were profoundly right in their conviction that it was not enough to say that Jesus was "of like substance" with the Father. To use the word "like" might mean that there was resemblance, yet not complete resemblance, so that there would be empty spaces in our faith. The Christian affirmation is that Jesus was "of one

147

substance" with the Father—"very God of very God." This means that over and above all present mysteries and our finite limitations, we can trust that here and hereafter we are in the hands of Him whose uncompromisingly holy purpose, whose unwearying outreach, whose mercy and forgiveness, are altogether such as that which we have seen in the life lived in Galilee and Jerusalem and in the illimitable redemptive power of the Cross. That is Christian theology at its deepest and its highest, and at the same time it is the message that comes closest to immediate human needs.

The final words of Paul's benediction, like the earlier ones, bring us back directly to those springs of experience from which flowed the later developed expressions of the creeds. It was and is the actual "fellowship of the Holy Spirit" which enables us to say, "I believe in the Holy Spirit." Since the days of the first disciples men have known the fact of that. Here again is a boundless area in which theological preaching may interpret life and be illuminated by life. All that a man can know about the history of the Church, about the mighty Christian figures in every generation, about the great communion of saints and heroes, can pour into the sort of preaching that makes faith relevant to the living day.

A right theology of the Holy Spirit should lead to direct and practical consequences. In the extreme forms of Barthian and neo-orthodox theology there is danger that the ethical aspects of true religion may be left unaccented. Sometimes young preachers are intimidated from preaching what seems to them both natural and needed by the disparaging comment that their sermons are "moralistic." The element of wholesome warning that is meant to find expression in that word is the realization that Christian salvation is something far more profound than satisfied observance of the poor little punctilios

148

of proper conduct. The greatness of the Holy Spirit, in relation to which all human pride must stand abased, has not entered into the man who thinks it is enough to attain a self-righteous respectability. That is true, but it is not true that ordinary morals do not greatly matter, and Christian theology should never be so slanted as even to suggest that. On the contrary "by their fruits ye shall know them." So the Master said, and the greatest of the apostles never forgot the intimate relationship between theology and everyday life. Read any one of Paul's epistles, even the most theological, and you will always come in its last pages to urgent and specific counsel as to how Christians should behave. That instant connection between the indwelling of the Spirit and ethical obedience must never be obscured. Faith without works is dead, and a living faith will show itself in a life that has the dignity of self-discipline and self-control, and that regards the plain injunctions of the Ten Commandments. Therefore the preacher who is the spokesman for the Word of God must deal in the course of his preaching with such concrete matters as personal moral behavior, the meaning of Christian marriage, the duties of responsible citizenship, and the standards which Christian public opinion must hold up for community conditions and for national policies in our interrelated world.

Thus theology, which is the attempt to understand and express the truth of what we may believe about God, leads to the parallel subject of what is to be expected of man. As to that relationship there have been clashes and contradictions in our human thought. Beginning with the Renaissance and in accelerating movement through the so-called Age of Enlightenment into the nineteenth century, the long Judaeo-Christian inheritance of faith in God was in process of being

149

dissipated. There was a growing revolt from any recognition of the supernatural. Increasingly it was assumed that man could be sufficient in himself and that the human race had grown so intelligent, so skillful and inventive, and so decently virtuous that it could shape its own destiny to its full satisfaction. The growth of that idea is evident to anyone who reads and remembers, and does not need to be elaborated. The result of it was the complacent conviction that God did not much matter and that human beings could get along well enough without bothering about whether he existed or not. This was heady wine for human pride, which could begin to announce, as A. C. Swinburne did, that

> Thou art smitten, thou God, thou art smitten; thy death
> is upon thee, O Lord.
> And the love-song of earth as thou diest resounds through the
> wind of her wings—
> Glory to Man in the highest! for Man is the master of things.[3]

But this idea of man as the master of everything was fated for disillusionment. Deprived of all sense of a divine relationship, men began to discover that they could lose both the strength and the incentive to master even themselves. What if the human being is forced to consider himself as some spokesmen of a bleak naturalism have described him?—an accident of evolution, a complex of reflexes, a mere by-product of chemical and physical processes that pursues his course across a fundamentally alien and brutal environment, and is doomed ultimately to finish his pointless journey with as little significance as belonged to the amoeba in which his ancestors once began it. There would not be much room for pride in *that*.

[3] From *The Hymn of Man*. Used by permission of Harper & Bros.

All the same, human arrogance, when it is aroused, dies hard. The twentieth century has seen it flame up into fierce expression. Hitler's Third Reich in Germany, with its boast that it would "last for a thousand years," was one mad effort to demonstrate that a man and a nation, gone pagan, could be stronger than any alleged laws of God or spiritual principles of humanity. In other countries and under different forms there has been and still can be essentially this same immoral arrogance. But the ashes of Berlin are not an isolated historical accident; they are the symbol of what must always happen when men ignore the fact that there is a moral order in the universe which brings doom to those who think they can defy it.

Human conduct and the recent history of its results have inevitably affected religious thinking. If formerly there was optimism about human nature, there is not much of it left. Voices that speak out of darkness, such as those of Kierkegaard and Barth, have been widely listened to. Their message is a warning of impending judgment, and the reason for it they put in old, blunt words that a complacent age had almost forgotten. Men are sinners—that is the stark fact. There are unbridled desires of the flesh, of the mind, and of the will. There is a lust for possessions and for power that destroys peace. And this rebellion against the right adjustment that was ordained for human life is so inveterate that theologians turn back to ground it again in the ancient doctrine of original sin. The story of Adam and Eve in the Garden is not read literally as it once was, but there is recognition that in that story there is expressed a truth so profound that it cannot be escaped—the truth that there is an evil of self-assertion which has involved the whole human race in its nature and consequences.

151

Contemporary people will listen thoughtfully to preaching which strikes that note. The powerful influence of interpreters like Niebuhr and Tillich in America and D. R. Davies in England has been evidence of that. Old types of evangelistic appeal related almost solely to the individual and his deliberate decisions and personal sins do not seem to go deep enough. Men feel themselves under the weight of corporate evils which cannot be lifted only by the individual's desire to repent. The preaching they want must be no casual, fair-weather "cheerio," but a message so full of understanding seriousness that it can reach them in the shadows where they are.

What are some of the aspects of the predicament of twentieth-century men that make its dimensions tragic?

1. First, there is a dismayed sense of the appalling power of the evil forces that can get loose in human life. A generation earlier, hardly anyone could have believed or even imagined the brutalities that have followed: obliteration bombing, the indiscriminate killing that dulled all pity, the fanatical race hatreds that tried to exterminate whole peoples, the obscene and bestial cruelties of Buchenwald. It was supposed that humanity had a clear future before it; instead it stands with dreadful awareness at the edge of an abyss. It was supposed that we had come a decisive distance on the road of moral evolution; instead, like Emperor Jones in Eugene O'Neill's play, we hear the increasing beat of the tom-toms of savage threats coming nearer and nearer in the jungle. Meanwhile it sometimes seems that a mass insanity is creeping in to overpower human reason and intelligent direction. Everybody knows that an atomic war might destroy all civilization, yet the nations go on stumbling toward it, like men caught in some blind hypnosis. No wonder that many

thinkers have begun to speak of evil forces that are demonic.

2. From this recognition of the power of evil there comes to many a shocked insecurity. Men are bewildered as to what, if anything, they can trust in. Old confidences are gone. Instead of anticipation for the future there is fear. "What is the use of planning for anything," young people ask themselves, "if the ground of a decent and dependable world is breaking up beneath us? If we could see ahead, it might be different. If we could know where we are going and are meant to go, we might summon up courage to ride out the storm." But they do not know. They feel like men on a fated ship for which day after day there is no sun and in the dark no stars to steer by. At length they are brought close to the kind of hopelessness which cries:

> What can we do, o'er whom the unbeholden
> Hangs in a night with which we cannot cope?[4]

3. The oppressive sense of the evil that is let loose and the resulting insecurity bring also what seems to be a shrinking of individual worth. One looks, for instance, at the moving-picture record of the rise of Nazism—the vast mobilization of black-shirted and brown-shirted masses in Munich or in Nuremberg, with the robot files goose-stepping, the massed drums rolling, and the heavy boots of the regimented thousands beating their hard rhythm past the frenzied shouting of the crowds. What can the individual do, and what can he amount to, a man may ask, when he is caught in the huge movement of the herd? And this impression of the individual's powerlessness, which can be so appalling when the force of

[4] Myers, op. cit., p. 14. Used by permission of St. Martin's Press, Inc.

the mass is dramatized, is felt also in a hundred less conspicuous but cumulative pressures of contemporary life. How
can my opinion count against what television and radio and
the chain newspapers are conveying to millions? What room
is there for independent thought and speech when intolerance
is ready to cramp everybody into its pattern? The world that
affects us has grown vaster, and by contrast the single person
seems that much more diminished. Once he lived as a free
and creative citizen in a community that was limited enough
to be manageable, but now the problems of both hemispheres
and of all countries press in upon him. It is an age of the
assembly line, both in work and in thought, with processes
too immense and complex for him to control. And so the
individual begins to think that he is only an insignificant cog
in the mechanism of human life, and he wonders whether
he has any significance for God.

4. Under the shadow of all the foregoing there comes to
people of the present time a possibility of the final and most
critical disillusionment. What if—when all is said and done
—we are "hollow men" in a hollow universe? If sometimes
there seems no discernible meaning in one's human existence,
may that be due to the fact that there is no meaning above
it? This uncertainty about any ultimate truth would leave
us with nothing to be loyal to. It would reduce life to something accidental and ephemeral and mean.

Such, then, are the needs that are waiting for a saving
gospel. As a student in an American university put it: "We
have been born into a world really browbeaten. The wonder
is that we have not lost faith in life itself during this period
of transition we are muddling through. Instead, we are restless,
skeptical, not knowing where to place our faith beyond half-

consciously wanting to find a consistency among these seeming conflicts. We are in a . . . destructive stage of antagonisms and immature emotions as to what to do next—but we want a dream and an ideal."

How shall Christian preachers bring a "dream and an ideal" —and more than a dream?

1. To a generation acutely aware of the force of evil in its world, the Christian preacher needs to come with understanding and to create confidence. With understanding—first. There will be no power in the man who shows that he has never himself confronted and wrestled with the stark realities by which all thoughtful persons must sometime be dismayed. But neither does he belong in the pulpit if, being there, he seems bent upon increasing the dismay that people already feel. No congregation wants to hear a perpetual Cassandra. Neither can a congregation stand a prophet every Sunday if their preacher's idea of being a prophet is to dwell continually on judgment and doom. There is a time for preaching judgment, but it is not all the time. His ultimate business is to make people become better, and they do not necessarily become better by being made to feel worse.

David H. C. Read was a chaplain with the British Army in 1939 and 1940, and also for the next five years was with the men of his division, but in a German internment camp for prisoners of war. He had plenty of acquaintance therefore with those grim and bitter aspects of reality that might suggest the wrath of God. But speaking after the war to other preachers he said:

You can hardly switch on a radio service without hearing someone dismally dissecting the body politic, or outlining the thought-processes of modern man. If you have a sermon that begins: "This

155

world is in a sorry state," I beseech you to burn it. In the first place, the average congregation does not believe that the minister knows how the modern man thinks: in the second place, they get very tired of this "modern man" and his near-relations, "the man in the street," "the average man," and "the world today," and would willingly exchange the lot for a flesh-and-blood man or woman whom we really know: and in the third place, our chief task as preachers is to be announcers of good news, not midwives of calamity.[5]

Yet preaching that seems to dwell upon calamity may be called orthodox, or neo-orthodox, and extolled as the saving influence from what is loosely disparaged as "outmoded liberal theology." There is, or was, a kind of liberalism which ought to be disparaged—the "liberalism" which was a complacent humanism, unconcerned with any great beliefs, shallow and spiritually cheap. But the fact that such "liberalism" deserves few defenders does not excuse the mechanical dogmatism which shudders at the adjective "liberal" as though even that would throw its piety out of gear. In its essence the liberal spirit in Christian faith is the spirit that is open-minded and therefore teachable, expectant, and courageous. It speaks in the words of a great old teacher which have become the motto of an American theological seminary: "Seek the truth, come whence it may, cost what it will." [6] It proclaims that there is a spring of potential heavenly energies put by God in the hearts of his human children that is meant to be not forgotten or relaxed. It has in it a dynamic which continually breaks through theological stereotypes, including the stereotype which seems to have fastened upon some mid-twentieth-century pulpits, that the more passionately it

[5] *The Communication of the Gospel*, p. 30. Used by permission of Student Christian Movement Press.

[6] Dr. William Sparrow, Virginia Theological Seminary.

is preached that men are in the grip of the devil, the more that preaching is to the glory of God.

What human souls need to be told is what Christian in *Pilgrim's Progress* needed to hear—not that there are dungeons in the Doubting Castle of Giant Despair, but, being in one, how to get out. Granted that the perils in our world are terrible. It is not the first time they have been so. The opportunity of the Christian preacher is to recall with glad encouragement God's saving acts in history, and to carry hope into the present and the future. Like the prophet Elisha, who opened the eyes of his frightened servant to see, beyond the forces that threatened them, the horses and chariots of fire (II Ki. 6:16-17), so the prophet of today is to make men know that "those who are with us are more than those who are with them."

2. What also is the message that Christian faith should bring to those who in a troubled time are haunted by insecurity? That message must ultimately be a strengthening answer, but before that it must be a question: What is security, and what sort of security do we want? The dictionary makes it plain that various shades of meaning may be in that one word. Security is "freedom from danger, risk, and so on." It is "freedom from care, apprehension, or doubt." Also it can be "something that secures or makes safe; a protection; a defense." Many people are seeking a security that will have in it all these aspects at once. Therefore some of them turn to Roman Catholicism, because they think that if they surrender to its monolithic and massive authority, they will get rid of the apprehension and doubt that they cannot deal with themselves. Others, who would never seek that hiding place, find another sort of refuge in a theology which,

157

though despondent about this present world, proclaims a salvation "at the end of history." But vital Christian preaching ought to sound a more challenging and a more inspiring note. It should assume that there is an essential gallantry in human souls that wants something better than a security which means "freedom from danger, risk, and so on." Certainly in the life of the spirit men must not be held incapable of the daring and determination which on great occasions they do superbly show. In 1950 two members of a French expedition scaled Annapurna in the Nepal Himalayas, the highest mountain which then had ever been climbed by man. That conquest was achieved through frightful hardships and at the cost for Maurice Herzog of the ultimate amputation of toes and fingers that had been frozen on the mountain. But the hazard he had carried through demonstrated "that there are still among us those who are willing to struggle greatly and suffer greatly for wholly ideal ends; for whom security is not the be-all and end-all of living; for whom there are conquests to be won in the world other than over their fellow men." [7] And Herzog himself, recuperating slowly in the hospital at Neuilly, wrote of himself and his companions: "Together we knew toil, joy and pain. . . . In my worst moments of anguish, . . . I saw that it was better to be true than to be strong. The marks of the ordeal are apparent on my body. I was saved and I had won my freedom. This freedom, which I shall never lose, has given me the assurance and serenity of a man who has fulfilled himself." [8]

A ship tied up in a dull harbor is out of danger; but only the ship that goes out to the risks of the sea is doing any-

[7] James Ramsey Ullman, "Trial by Ice," *Life*, July 9, 1951.

[8] Maurice Herzog, *Annapurna* (New York: E. P. Dutton & Co., 1953), p. 12.

thing. So it is with people, and so the Christian preacher must proclaim that concern for the wrong kind of security can become an obsession which is ignominious. The true security comes not from a frightened search for it, but as a by-product of something greater. It is the inner security that belongs to those who are steadfast in some clear commitment and in the strength of that find "freedom from care, apprehension, or doubt."

Moreover it is true that the brave man who goes out beyond where there is safety is not likely to find himself alone. Herzog was not alone on Annapurna. The great quest will bring men together as companions. In the enterprises of the spirit Christians can remember that they can be part of the spiritual company of the Church that sets out—as the Pilgrims did— on the great adventure of a living purpose which has its risks and dangers, but also has the power of believing that its fulfillment is safe in the hands of God.

3. Directly related to this must be preaching that lifts up the sense of individual worth which so many men and women are in danger of losing. It is a deadly falsehood to think or act as though the world's condition had brought it about that for the individual this is no longer a "time for greatness." Now, as always, God has his high purposes for ordinary men and women to carry out. As these words are written, one of the most valued of all public awards, the Pulitzer award for distinguished service in journalism, has been given to two weekly country newspapers of five thousand and less than two thousand circulation in Whiteville and Tabor City, small towns of North Carolina.[9] Columbus County in that state had been terrorized by the lawless violence of a Ku Klux

[9] *Time,* May 11, 1953, p. 51.

Klan. People had been dragged out of their houses at the whim of the hooded night riders, flogged and threatened with more flogging if they dared resist. Decent people were ashamed at what was happening in their community, but most of them only said, "What can anybody do?" Then the editors of the two little newspapers gave the answer. Week by week despite the danger they knew they ran they told on their front pages every detail they could uncover about the Klan and about who might be in its secret ranks. At length they stirred the laggard law-enforcement agencies into action; members of the Klan were identified, arrested, and indicted; the leaders were sent to jail, and the whole brutal business put an end to. That was what two individuals achieved.

The courage and the moral confidence those two men showed are acutely needed in every Christian country and community—and needed all the more because they have been too little expected. There has grown a kind of corrosive doubt as to what men can accomplish, a doubt that may be most evident in the countries where it ought to be impossible: namely, in those that have a civilization which at least in its heritage and in its continuing desire is Christian. It is truly said that the gospel is not tied to any particular form of human politics, nor would the best of such forms ever be equivalent to the kingdom of God; but all the same it is a dangerous fact that in the most anti-Christian countries where Communist dogma is contemptuous of the dignity of the individual there is nevertheless an enormous confidence in the total power of men to mold their world. The fanatical dynamism of Russia and of Communist China has no doubts or hesitations. It is passionately sure that the future is in its hands. Indeed the proximate future might be in its hands if the peoples who ought to believe in the worth and power of every individual

160

soul should lose the force of their own conviction and should prove unworthy of their spiritual heritage. The ultimate future would still belong to him who sits above the circle of the earth, to whom its inhabitants are like grasshoppers, its nations like a drop from a bucket, and its rulers as nothing (Isa. 40); for his final purposes are not tied to any particular form of human government or politics. But the immediate opportunity God has meant for Christian people would be forfeited if they no longer had the faith, the invincible patience, and the consecrated will which a perilous time demands.

That is why there is mortal danger in the subtle defeatism which can be created by the very orthodoxy which dwells—but may dwell one-sidedly—upon its message of the sovereignty and judgment of God. God is sovereign, but his decisive sovereignty may want to exercise itself through human individuals alert enough and brave enough to be his instruments. A world in crisis cannot be saved by a pessimistic and paralyzing theology which disintegrates belief in what men can do. We need instead the kind of preaching which will be a flame of faith—faith that Christian men and women, in their churches and as citizens, under God can make a better world. On a divine level Christians as defenders of moral and spiritual reality may well remember what Konstantine Simonov in his *Days and Nights*, put upon the lips of a common soldier. In the siege of the city upon which at that moment the fate of many nations hung, one of the desperate defenders, looking out upon the attacking forces, said to the man at his side, "They don't give any date when they will take Stalingrad. . . . What is the reason?" And the man replied, "We are the reason." So in reply to the question why God's spiritual purpose for his world shall not be overrun, let individual Christians dare to say, "We are the reason!"

161

4. At the heart of all that has been said is of course the fact that contemporary preaching must reinforce faith in the living God. This it will best do not by arguments and esoteric language, but rather by calling upon men and women to go out into life and put their faith to the test. It is by acting as though the higher power were with them that Christians gain the inner courage and assurance that makes them know the heavenly power is real. The memorable words quoted by King George VI of England in his Christmas broadcast in the dark year of 1939 are greatly true:

I said to the man who stood at the gate of the year:
"Give me a light, that I may tread safely into the unknown!"
And he replied:
"Go out into the darkness and put your hand into the Hand of God.
That shall be to you better than light and safer than a known way." [10]

SUGGESTIONS FOR SUPPLEMENTARY READING

Farmer, Herbert H. *Servant of the Word*. New York: Chas. Scribner's Sons, 1942.

McCracken, Robert J. *Questions People Ask*. New York: Harper & Bros., 1951.

McIntyre, R. E. *The Ministry of the Word*. New York: Thomas Nelson & Sons, 1950.

Read, David H. C. *The Communication of the Gospel*. London: Student Christian Movement Press, 1952.

Wedel, Theodore O. *The Christianity of Main Street*. New York: The Macmillan Co., 1950.

[10] From "The Gate of the Year" by M. Louise Haskins. Used by permission of Christy & Moore, Ltd.

CHAPTER NINE

Constructing the Sermon

IN THE FIRST WORDS of Chapter Four it was said that the time to begin a sermon is long before it has to begin. The meaning of that should have grown clear in all that was then considered. True preaching is no hasty and shallow utterance. It must be drawn from reservoirs of thought and purpose long fed from many springs.

But the moment comes when a man must sit down and get his sermon ready. From out of all that he knows and feels he must prepare something to say in particular expression at an immediate time. How shall he go about his work?

First, he will remember that what he is to do is to bring God's truth to God's people; and the stimulus for his sermon may come from either end. He may have primarily in his mind some high suggestion from the Bible which he has already read and pondered, and which he wants to make relevant for human lives. Or, instead, he may be thinking of some special human need which his pastoral contacts have made him understand; and he is seeking for the truth which will bring its answer to that need.

The classical preaching of earlier times began mostly in the former way. So it was with men like John Wesley, Frederick W. Robertson, Henry Ward Beecher, Phillips Brooks. They were oriented toward the Bible. They lifted their eyes,

163

and therefore they lifted the eyes of a congregation, toward eternal truths, as one might stand and gaze at some majestic alpine peak shining in its white glory against the sky. So to stand, in awed contemplation, hushed and reverent, is in itself to bring enlargement to the soul. But that is not all. The great truths are not isolated and unrelated. On the contrary, when men have regarded those truths as they are ranged before them in the Scriptures, they perceive that they are like the mountains in another way. From their clouds and snows the waters condense, and from their mighty heights the rivers flow down to fertilize and refresh the valleys of men's needs.

So the preacher of today may begin with the Bible and know that his preaching may thus be framed in great dimensions. That can be true whether he is dealing with a single text or with some longer passage of scripture. In either case, if he has caught a glimpse of the grandeur of the meaning of God, he will have helped to make his people conscious of the loftiness to which their own lives are related.

Or it may be, on the other hand—and this is characteristic of much contemporary preaching—that a man's thought is quickened first by some particular and urgent human fact. Here are people—people in perplexity, people who are lost and do not know where to go. It is upon *them* that his consideration centers and by *them* and not immediately by some impulse from the Bible that he is moved to preach. He sees them like men lost in a desert, in mortal thirst. They have followed supposed paths that led nowhere, false hopes that ended as a mirage. With all the power of his compassion he wants to come to aid them. But how shall he do it? Not by merely *wanting* to. That is not enough. No analysis of their plight and no amount of genial chatter—which are all that some preaching is—will be enough. He must know where

164

the oasis is, and the only oasis that can satisfy men's thirst and save them is where the waters of God's truth are welling up. It is to this that the preacher must lead the thirsty people. Thus his text may come at the end of his sermon instead of at the beginning. Because he has started where the people are, his sermon may be called a "life-situation sermon"; but its ultimate message is biblical. In every sermon which is to be enriching the two realities must be married: the truth of God and the need of man. The one prerequisite is that the preacher must have in his mind and heart something that has become intensely real to him, whether it is some thrilling awareness of an aspect of God's truth which has burst into light for him as he sat reading his Bible and which he then wants to translate into its relevance for life, or whether it has come from a perception of human wistfulness so poignant that he searches his Bible to find its answer.

It is this intensity of purpose and consequent urgency that makes the difference among men and causes one man in the ministry to advance in spiritual power while another retrogrades. Everyone who has watched thoughtfully the progress of groups who graduate from a seminary will have noted a fact which at first seemed strange and contradictory—namely, that some of the men whose natural abilities appeared to give the brightest promise fail, as the years go on, to exert any significant influence from their pulpits; while other men of apparently ordinary attainments become preachers of authority and power. The reason is that the men of the first kind succumb to the temptation of preaching from the glancing but superficial pools of easy ideas, while the other men sink deep shafts down to the bedrock of their convictions in order to strike the living water. These latter men may never learn to preach sermons which are prettily arranged, like a

165

tinkling fountain in a well-ordered garden; but there may be an elemental power in their preaching like the gushing of an artesian well. Those who listen to them feel that men like these and the sermons they preach are real, and it is reality that people want to hear.

Suppose then that a man knows why he wants to preach and what he wants to preach about. Then he faces the question of how he is to construct his sermon so as to accomplish effectively what he seeks to do. That means work: thoughtful, disciplined, patient, and exact. And it is just at this point that many men fail. They would like so much to find an easier way. Some students in theological seminaries, and apparently some older men also, approach the construction of their sermons with a cheerful belief in the nebular hypothesis of creation. Scientists tell us that this earth of ours was formed by the gradual solidifying of a huge mass of inchoate gas. That process did succeed in forming a very pleasant earth, but it took a long time. It is conceivable that if a man who is about to write a sermon had time enough, he could somehow get one to evolve out of the whirling nebula of rotating notions; but the fact is that he does not have aeons at his disposal. He must get that sermon finished in a day or two, and in that space of time what begins as a nebula will still be only nebulous. As a matter of fact, this is exactly what happens with a great many preachers. They have an idea, and then they "just sit down and begin to write." The result is that the sermon goes trailing along, curling perhaps into pretty words here and there, but altogether insubstantial, so that the listener on Sunday who grasps at it for some solid fact will find nothing there in the midst of its beguiling vapor.

If a sermon is to stand up, it must have structure. Its purpose may come from a breathing of the Holy Spirit, but the Spirit is not conveyed best by carelessness. The preacher is subject to requirements not less than those which every other creator in the realm of thought must recognize. The artist may have his sudden perception of some new beauty, but he cannot embody it unless he has mastered the technique of line and color. The musician cannot create his symphony until he can bring all the elements of his orchestra into right relationship to the motif his inner ear has heard. The architect may have a vision of some noble house, but in order to build it and to make it fit to live in, he must work out the slow and intricate exactness of the blueprints. And as the blueprint is imperative for the architect, so the fashioning of a sermon outline is imperative for the man who has to preach. He must not merely trust to his ability to say something; he must know what he wants to say and plan unerringly how to say it.

The shaping of the sermon's structure must be neither too early nor too late. The preacher who begins right off to try to hammer out a worried mechanical pattern into which his thought must fit has put this whole effort too early. And the preacher who drifts into the writing of a scrambling, structureless sermon and then extracts from it some memoranda which he calls an outline has come to this so late that the sense has gone out of it altogether. What ought to happen is that the sermon structure should begin to develop spontaneously out of the preacher's conscious and subconscious brooding upon his sermon theme. That theme ought to be in his mind soon enough for him to think unhurriedly about it, with the sort of thinking that is not a behind-schedule cudgeling of his brains, but a meditation which can go on at odd moments as well as when he is in his study. A whole assortment of ideas will start to gather: questions, possible answers, sudden and un-

167

foreseen associations, recollections of something read or of something seen that may be illustrative. The brain paths are alerted, and whatever material is there starts to move up to the point of call. Jot down these thoughts freely and simply, with no concern at first for strict order. Then presently they will begin to take form of themselves. Some of them will be laid aside as not directly relevant. Others will coalesce into logical sequences that progressively appear.

"All of which is understandable in general," a man may say, "but what does it mean in specific illustration?"

Take then the possibility that one who is to preach has happened to be arrested in his reading of the Bible by what may seem at first to be only an incidental phrase. In the ninth chapter of the Gospel of Luke there is the account of how Jesus and his disciples on their way to Jerusalem came to the gates of a little Samaritan town, sought harborage for the night, and were refused. Then what happened? Only this: "They went to another village."

What important suggestion is there in that? At first there may seem to be none. The obvious fact is merely that Jesus and his disciples did not enter where he had meant to enter, but went away. The people of the first village did not care. There was nothing that they thought they needed to regret.

But then for the preacher the questions begin to wake. Was the failure of the Samaritan villagers all the more disastrous because they never knew there had been any failure? Is that the way it is with life? May its most awful deprivations be those which we do not recognize? Jesus knocks at the gates of our hearts, as he knocked at the gates of the Samaritan village; and we do not let him in. Why not? And what happened when he was refused—and what happens now? No
168

angry punishment, but only the fact of people left to their own mean isolation. But may that be the most awful of all penalties—this self-chosen penalty of life content with its own littleness? And may the meaning of hell be the waking up at last to what has been lost, when it is too late?

Such are some of the wonderings which gather round that gospel incident. Out of it may develop a sermon on "When Christ Passes By," with a structure that develops thus from the text "They went to another village."

Introduction:
Here in the words that seem so brief and unimportant there is embodied one of the deepest facts with which you or I could possibly be concerned. For here is a picture of lives which have lost their opportunity.
  I. The story of the Samaritan village, not only as an incident in the Gospel, but as a parallel of all human souls.
    A. (1) The messengers of Jesus came to the village gates and were rebuffed.
      (2) Jesus was there to give the people of that village everything he had to give, and they would not take it.
      (3) He did not call down fire from heaven, as James and John desired. He did not seem to leave the Samaritans punished at all.
      (4) They were entirely satisfied. But meanwhile what might have happened would not happen there: sick people healed by Jesus' touch, little children blessed, the discouraged inspired, men who were sinners quickened to a new life. The punishment was in the complacency and spiritual stagnation to which the village had condemned itself, so that what might have been would never be.
    B. (1) To the gates of human hearts likewise Jesus comes.
      (2) If refusal of him led to some immediate demonstration of the wrath of God, we might be shocked into awareness.

169

       (3) But that is not the way of God in Jesus. He simply spreads before us the facts of life and waits for us to look and understand and choose.

       (4) And if we refuse, we may learn the reality of hell—the spiritual hell whose characteristic is not so much what it contains as what it lacks, a hell of ultimate emptiness and disillusionment and self-contempt.

II. Why did the Samaritans reject Jesus, and why may we?

  A. Because his messengers represented something new and unexpected.

       (1) The Samaritans moved in a groove of stodgy habit. They did not want to bother with strangers.

       (2) So we today in regard to social, economic, or religious inheritance and habit may rebuff the word of Jesus which demands thinking that is new.

  B. Because Jesus and his disciples were aliens.

       (1) The Samaritans did not look at their visitors as particular individuals. They looked upon them as Jews; they did not like Jews, and that closed the matter.

       (2) So men in every time may reject the approaches of Christ's spirit because these conflict with their prejudices. For example:

          The scorn of the Church of England for John Wesley and the Methodist revival.

          The early contempt for the modern missionary movement.

          The resistance to appeals for social justice if they come from classes or members of a race that reactionary conservatism suspects.

  C. Because Jesus and his disciples were unimpressive.

       (1) To the Samaritans they did not look like persons of importance.

       (2) And again the Christian challenge may be scorned if it comes as the lonely word of unfashionable truth; as the suggestion of some better cause of action which the crowd at first will laugh at; as the religious evangel which does not start in high places, but grows up among simple and heart-hungry folk.

III. Yet the final thought must go beyond the picture of failure. What if the Samaritan village *had* welcomed Jesus? What if we welcome him now? He comes to bring love and life.

A. The spirit of love.

    (1) There are people who are spiritually dying because their sympathies continually contract, their tempers grow acid, their spirits morbid and mean.

    (2) But those who keep the gates of their sympathies wide open to the world are those who consciously or unconsciously welcome Christ, and the love of God comes in to bless.

B. Greatness of life.

    Only as there is recognition of the best and truest in life around us can there be abundance of life within.

Conclusion:

As in Galilee and Samaria there were places which Christ had to pass by, so there were places where he found welcome. Of which sort are we when he comes to the gates of human hearts?

A young preacher-in-process was wrestling once with the description in the tenth chapter of Mark of James and John coming to Jesus and asking for places of honor in his kingdom, and he tried unsuccessfully to make an effective sermon out of it. He saw that their original ambition was selfish. He noted Jesus' rebuke and that he offered them not honors, but risk and persecution, so that one of them would be martyred and the other would die unnoticed by the world. But he glimpsed the fact that these men, known now to all history for their ultimate witness to their Lord, reached something higher than the thrones they coveted. So at length he found his sermon, of how lives that really want to learn of Christ can be lifted into greatness. And his ultimate message is instantly suggested by his three final heads:

I. What James and John wanted

II. The contrasting fact of what James and John got
III. Yet what James and John got was what they wanted—but transfigured

Let it be remembered that there is no stereotype for a sermon structure. It should be a living thing, growing naturally within the body of the thought and directly adapted to it. But there are certain familiar forms which can be guides to a man's imagination and one or another of which may instinctively seem to him most right for a particular sermon.

Frederick W. Robertson, one of the greatest of all English-speaking preachers, had an almost invariable habit of creating his sermons according to two main divisions. He would present one side of the truth and then turn it about and show the other, like two hemispheres that make up the global whole. For example, he preached on the "Transitoriness of Life" and divided it thus:

I. The feelings suggested by a retrospect of the past
II. The right direction of those feelings

Or consider his famous sermon on Elijah as he fled into the wilderness and "requested for himself that he might die," and observe its extraordinary co-ordination and balance. Beginning with the vivid suggestion that sometimes a man's most signal failure may take place at the point where generally he is most strong, he shows Elijah, "this man, so stern, so iron, so independent," yet giving way in his trial hour "to a fit of petulance and querulous despondency to which there is scarcely found a parallel." Then—not only concerning Elijah but with reference to all human souls—Robertson makes clear what he wants to speak to: "Religious despondency, therefore, is our subject." And here, abbreviated, is his outline:

 I. The causes of Elijah's despondency
   A. Relaxation of physical strength
   B. Want of sympathy. "I, even I only, am left."
   C. Want of occupation
   D. Disappointment in the expectation of success
II. God's treatment of that despondency
   A. God recruits his servant's exhausted strength. (He feeds him.)
   B. God calms Elijah's stormy mind by the healing influences of nature.
   C. God makes him feel the earnestness of life. "What doest thou here, Elijah?" Life is for doing—and the prophet was not doing but moaning.
   D. God completes the cure by the assurance of victory. "Yet I have left me seven thousand in Israel, all the knees which have not bowed unto Baal." They had been braced and encouraged by his example, and so in God's world for those who are in earnest there is no failure.[1]

Another pattern which can often be extraordinarily effective in the help it gives to the preacher's own mind as he tries to block his material out is the pattern of a drama. Most effective plays are in three acts, and by the same analogy many of the most effective sermons are arranged in three main divisions. The first division in the sermon, like the first act of a play, will reveal a particular situation. The second division, like the second act, will introduce a growing complication; and the third division, like the third act, will bring the illumination of what up to that point has been contradictory and confused. The advantage of this picture in the preacher's mind is that it will help to bring into his sermon the elements of suspense, of growing interest, and of climax. Sermons which deal with the great figures of the Bible, or

[1] *Sermons on Bible Subjects,* Everyman's Library. Used by permission of E. P. Dutton & Co. and J. M. Dent & Sons, Ltd.

with some tense incident in those exciting stories of which the Bible is so full, fall instinctively into this pattern.

Take, for example, that arresting exclamation in the thirty-seventh chapter of Genesis (R.S.V.), "Here comes this dreamer." Here, indeed, begins the great drama of a human soul in its relation to God and to men, and the sequence of it for a sermon may run thus:

I. The opening scene, with its contrast between the elder sons of Jacob and the dreamer Joseph.
   A. The elder brothers, hard-handed, narrow-minded men, who considered themselves to be the realists, despised the brother they thought was only a visionary boy.
   B. And what of Joseph?
      (1) His strength was that he had wide imagination and a great sense that life could be large and wonderful.
      (2) His weakness was that his imaginations were self-centered. Consider the nature of his dreams.
II. The second scene, in which Joseph is put to the test.
   From his inherited religion and from his own confidence he had believed that God had a meaning for his life. But now—
   A. These are the shattering facts:
      He was sold as a slave;
      Tempted by Potiphar's wife and then lyingly accused;
      Put into prison;
      Forgotten by the fellow prisoners whom he had befriended.
   B. What might have happened?
      He could have abandoned his dreams of greatness in bitter disillusionment;
      He could have believed that God had deserted him, that life had no decent meaning, and that if scrapping his ideals and even his morality would help him get ahead, then—as with Potiphar's wife—let him be immoral.
   C. What did happen?
      In the teeth of tempting circumstances Joseph kept his

honor and his religious loyalty—"How then can I do this great wickedness, and sin against God?"

III. The final scene of vindication.

When his brothers came down to Egypt, they found this Joseph whom they had sold as a slave seated now on Pharaoh's viceregal throne. He was the "dreamer," whom they had despised, but not the same dreamer as at first, for—

A. His concern with dreams was no longer selfish. He had interpreted Pharaoh's dream and become the servant and deliverer of a people.

B. He had seen the ways of God in a mightier perspective. Looking back upon all he had passed through, he could say superbly to his brothers, "It was not you that sent me here, but God."

It is possible that the shaping of an outline in this fashion, which gives it some element of dramatic progress and mounting interest, may be still more sharply illustrated by the contrast between the groping beginnings of an outline and the more coherent form in which it is finally worked out. A seminary student essayed to preach one day on the "Meaning of Greatness." He took as his text the description in the twenty-eighth chapter of the First Book of Samuel of the women of Israel welcoming King Saul and David after their victory over the Philistines, and chanting, to Saul's infinite annoyance, "Saul hath slain his thousands, and David his ten thousands."

I. Our ideas of greatness and those of the past
    Hero worship, receptions, etc.
    Lindbergh and David

II. Recognizing greatness in others
    Saul's attitude toward David
    David's attitude toward Saul

III. What should be our attitude as Christians?
    Lessons from Christ
    Examples of magnanimity

IV. How should we measure greatness?
   Not by external values
   Not by wealth and friends
   But by character, good deeds, etc.

One glance at this outline will show that it is wholly lacking in any considered pattern, unless it is such a pattern as a boy uses when he makes a kite's tail—a succession of rags tied one below the other and united by nothing but a thin string which jerks and wriggles in the wind. There is no sure progress and certainly no inevitability in the succession of ideas. Almost any rearrangement of the four main points would be as logical and sensible as the arrangement which happens to have been arrived at.

It is obvious too that the preacher has completely overlooked the dramatic possibilities of his theme, with all the vivid and kindling interest which this could create. He does, it is true, have a fugitive glimpse of this possibility, for he has spoken of "Saul's attitude toward David" and "David's attitude toward Saul"; but these are only incidental subdivisions. He has spoken too of the "lessons from Christ," but this also is merely an idea dropped almost accidentally into a subdivision and never lifted into any sharp definiteness.

The problem was not to write another sermon, but to take the material he already had and the ideas which were implicit in his confused arrangement and to bring these into clear, effective focus.

Here is the way in which the outline was refashioned. The wording of it is different. Some new material has been added, but in such a way as not to make a different sermon, but to make clear the "Measure of Greatness," which was what the preacher in the first place wanted to interpret.

Introduction. A brief summary of the biblical passage

I. The crowd's estimate of greatness

A crude measurement of numbers, bulk, size

The great man in the primitive estimate was the man who could kill the most enemies.

Our own reversion to that in the time of war

In business the man who outstrips his rivals, who accummulates and amasses for himself

The measurement which has to do with outward signs and not with inner facts

II. Saul's and David's estimates

A. Saul follows the crowd idea, believes in a success which must be guaranteed for him by rewards and recognition

Wants to keep the spoils from Amalek

Ambitious at all costs to keep the kingdom for himself and his dynasty

The consequent envy and hate against David, who seems to be his rival

B. David

His thought of the right thing to be done, rather than of his own fortunes

His desire to serve Saul

His magnanimity toward him—toward his family

II Sam. 9

His love for Absalom

A man who in spite of grave shortcomings and sins tried to set his life humbly before the judgment of the greatness of God—and in that found his ultimate inner greatness

III. Greatness as revealed in Christ

The best that was in David as a hint of what Christ incarnated

His greatness of service—"Not to be ministered unto, but to minister"

It will be plain that a sermon preached from the second outline would be accompanied with a far greater clearness and confidence in the mind of the preacher himself and would command the attention of the congregation in a far surer way than the first outline ever could have done.

A sermon structure with three main divisions, as illustrated in the outlines reviewed, has some definite advantages. The three main points are enough to give room for evident movement and progress of thought, and yet few enough for the listeners to grasp and to remember. Their relationship can be set forth, as was suggested in the sermon on Joseph, in a sequence that is dramatic; or they can be conceived in the familiar logical terms of thesis, antithesis, and synthesis.

But there is of course nothing sacrosanct about a three-point or two-point principle of structure. The pattern of a sermon may grow directly out of its text. A sermon, for example, on the vision in the book of Revelation of the Holy City coming down out of heaven from God and built foursquare upon the earth, with gates to the east and north and south and west, through which the nations of the earth will bring their treasures, will almost inevitably fall into a four-fold development, as one considers it as a symbol of the gifts of the meditative east, the progressive north, the romantic south, and the practical west, all alike brought into the fullness of the meaning of God's purpose for mankind. So also an expository sermon, such as the one by Henry Sloane Coffin summarized in Chapter Seven, will include as many points as the thought may naturally make dominant. The so-called expository sermon is the same as a sermon built upon a single brief text in that the purpose of each is to make clear the great facets of truth in the Bible's words. The difference is that an expository sermon deals with a longer passage of scripture and requires therefore more analysis and a discriminating choice as to those elements on which emphasis should fall. Real exposition is not a mechanical string of comments upon

178

all the words and verses in a Bible passage—neither upon all of them, nor necessarily upon those chosen in their printed order. The mark of the interpreter's insight is the ability to grasp the dominant and unitive truth of a whole passage and then to perceive and to express those aspects of it which set the truth in its most sure perspective.

Thus giving structure to a sermon is a living and flexible matter. Various forms are possible, and any one of these may prove the most effective for a particular sermon. Halford E. Luccock in that book of his by which every preacher can find his thought quickened, *In the Minister's Workshop*, has illustrated this rich variety. A sermon may be constructed throughout on some vivid analogy, drawn from nature or from life. (Consider, for example, Jesus' parable of the sower.) It may be developed according to the principle of classification. Here is a problem to be met. What are the ways in which a man might try to meet it, which ways are wrong and why, and which alone is right? Or the sermon may proceed as would a debate. Here is the proclamation of what is to be maintained as truth: the reason why it is to be held as true, recognition and rebuttal of the arguments that may be brought against it, and a final appeal to accept the truth and act upon it. Or the sermon may follow that method of persuasion which appears in William James's "ladder of faith," in which the reasoning begins upon the solid ground of recognition concerning "some momentous view of life or of the world, or of religion, that it is a possible view, it is not self-contradictory, it is not absurd." Then the next step upward is to see that "it *might* well be true as far as the actual facts are concerned," then in succession that "it *may* be true now," "it is *fit* to be true," "it *ought* to be true," and "we affirm it *must* be true." So in the gallant words of William James's conclusion, "We

179

say at the top of the ladder, it *shall* be true, at any rate for me, because I am going to adopt it as my truth and live by it henceforth."

All these and many other possible forms of sermon structure are to be as servants, not masters. No one of them is to become a compulsion or a habit. The artist does not go on painting the same picture over and over again. The architect does not plan all his buildings alike. He uses his creative imagination each time to construct what will be most fitting and most beautiful for the purpose he has in mind. And so it should be with the man who is to construct the sermon that is meant to body forth some aspect of God's truth here on the ground of human life. Now and then a sermon may develop with a spontaneity that seems to transcend any pattern that the preacher has followed before, as was true in one of the noblest sermons of its decade, John Haynes Holmes's "The Unknown Soldier Speaks." It was an imaginative dialogue between the preacher and the Unknown Soldier from his tomb. It had in it the freedom and inevitability of great poetry. Its thought began and mounted and enlarged like a wind-blown flame. And in this same way some inspiring theme may give to any preacher a sudden and thrilling newness of conception as to how the truth at that moment should be expressed.

So when all is said, a double fact appears. On the one hand, a preacher is never to think of sermon structure as one or another cast-iron mold into which his thought is to be compressed. He is engaged in what is a living art, not in the process of an assembly line. But on the other hand, he will be foolish to act as though experience and knowledge begin with him. The patterns which have been used by generations

180

of preachers are not arbitrary, but they do have authority—the authority of what has long been put to the proof. The point of central importance for the preacher in any period is that he should combine freedom of spirit with teachableness in technique. His own mind may more surely find its way ahead if he knows the directions which others have marked out. And he can depend upon it that the more clear and direct is the organization of his sermon, the more certainly the understanding of his congregation will follow where he wants it to go. For a sermon to give

to the hearers continuous clues to what it is all about . . . is an eminently reasonable service. . . . Stages of movement, definitely announced, clarify the mental trip as helpfully as do the announcements of the railroad conductor when he calls out, "This station is Utica; the next stop is Syracuse." That may be stooping to a lowly service, but it does serve the traveler in a way that no eloquence alone could match.[2]

SUGGESTIONS FOR SUPPLEMENTARY READING

Brown, Charles R. *The Art of Preaching.* New York: The Macmillan Co., 1922.

Coffin, Henry Sloane. *Communion Through Preaching.* New York: Chas. Scribner's Sons, 1952.

Luccock, Halford E. *In the Minister's Workshop.* New York and Nashville: Abingdon Press, 1944.

Morris, Frederick M. *How to Preach Effectively.* New York: Morehouse-Gorham Co., Inc., 1954.

Newton, Joseph Fort. *If I Had Only One Sermon to Prepare.* New York: Harper & Bros., 1932.

Sangster, W. E. *The Craft of Sermon Construction.* Philadelphia: Westminster Press, 1951.

Stevenson, Dwight E. *A Guide to Expository Preaching.* Lexington, Ky.: College of the Bible, 1952.

———. *A Road Map for Sermons.* Lexington, Ky.: College of the Bible, 1950.

[2] Luccock, *op. cit.*, p. 120.

181

CHAPTER TEN

More About Sermon Construction

SUPPOSE THE PREACHER has brooded over his sermon until its message and purpose are alive in his mind and imagination, and the structure of it has begun to take instinctive shape. Then what?

Then he should sit down, as early in the week as possible, to write it out, carefully and completely. Whether he will ultimately read the manuscript from the pulpit is another matter, which will be considered presently. But certainly in the early years of his ministry, and perhaps for as long as he lives, he should work out on paper what he intends to say. Thereby he safeguards himself from the shallowness and thinness which will mark the preaching of the man who assumes that a few hasty notes and a possible glibness of speech are enough to equip him to deliver a message from God. Writing his sermons, with the steady, patient, and often taxing work which that entails, is his first tribute to the high and holy responsibility he bears to God and to his people. Time is life, and the people who have given a part of their time to sit silent in the pews and listen to a preacher are giving him part of their life, which he dare not treat casually nor dismiss with some slovenly offering on his part. A man who takes

182

his message seriously in any sphere of human concern will want to prepare what he is going to say, and if it is a great occasion, he will prepare, perhaps, for long hours and days of concentrated mental labor. The man who is championing some social cause will do that. The leader in some critical civic or political movement will do it. They do not leave results to chance, because the issue they are concerned with is too important. What, then, of the issue with which the preacher deals? Let him not suffer the familiarity and frequency of preaching to dull for him its divine urgency. His business is to make God clear to men, and he cheapens all his prophethood if he ever suffers himself to drift into the lazy habit of preaching without the truest preparation which time and strength and disciplined intelligence will allow.

Writing a sermon compels a man to discover whether he is really thinking his subject through or whether he is only pretending to think and fooling himself (though not ultimately his congregation) with the idea that he has created a message with a backbone in it when he has only produced a few jellyfish notions that might be kept afloat in a sea of words. The written sermon is an inexorable mirror. Once it is finished, a man may look at it and take the measure of his own intellectual processes. Before he goes into the pulpit, he can know whether or not he has anything substantial to say and whether also he has so expressed it that the sermon will convey its thought to the listeners on Sunday as surely and as strongly as is possible for him. This means that he must use all the skill he possesses or can develop in the plain matter of making the English language his effective tool.

It is true that there will be an inclination in some men— and perhaps in nearly every man sometime—to balk at that. "Must we get involved in a lot of matters of technique?" they

183

ask. "If a man really has something he genuinely wants to say, why can't he just get up and say it as well as he can?" And the answer is that "as well as he can" and as well as the people deserve can never come out of indifference or negligence. A sermon *is* primarily a thing of the spirit, and the instinct is right which is concerned lest it be caught in mechanics which would keep it from being spontaneous. But spontaneity which is not enriched by much thought and controlled by steady purpose can become a mere verbal sputter. A sermon is born out of a glow in the preacher's mind and heart, and without that glow even the best technique would leave it drab and cold; but the general glow is not enough. The thought and spirit of the sermon must be so refined, so purified, and so directed that they become a clear and shining light to make men glad with the distinctness of its illumination.

In the last century in England there rose a great man who by his genius brought new and uplifting influence to what was then the very harsh and dark tradition of the English public schools. Edward Thring of Uppingham believed that boys could be developed only in a school which by its every feature appealed to all that was best in them. He wrote:

I lay claim to have been great as a schoolmaster on this, and on this only, in the main; on having had the sense to work with tools, to follow God's guidance in teaching beginners by surrounding them, as He did, with noble and worthy surroundings, taking care that there was no meanness or neglect. . . . It is a slow process, but it is a true one; it is not grand, but it is practical; it needs patience, but it works by degrees higher life. I take my stand on detail.[1]

[1] G. R. Parkin, *Life and Letters of Edward Thring* (London: Macmillan Co., 1910), pp. 222, 223.

Every preacher may well follow that idea of Thring's. He must not be ashamed of detail, not ashamed but proud to have the "sense to work with tools," to fashion every sentence which he is speaking to people in God's name with the utmost precision and artistry he can attain.

There are simple principles which will help a man appraise, and try to perfect, the details of his sermon. He should have constantly in the back of his mind these questions:
Is it clear?
Is it interesting and significant?
Is it vivid?
Is it convincing?

1. Is it clear? Obviously that question comes first. Unless a man knows what he is driving at, his congregation is certainly not likely to know. Neither will it do for him to have a benevolent or general aim but with no sure and steadying concentration. The man who takes a vaguely inclusive glance at the whole target and shoots at its indiscriminate bulk is likely to miss the target altogether and to have his arrow lose itself in the woods beyond it. If, on the other hand, he looks at the bull's-eye with such concentration that every energy is co-ordinated in planting his arrow *there,* he may not succeed even then in hitting squarely in the center; but he will come a great·deal nearer to it than if he had not tried so definitely. In the same way the man who is to preach must see clearly what is the heart of the thing he is aiming at. He must know what is the one significant aspect of truth which through this particular sermon he is trying to reach with the arrow of his thought. And he must so shape his sermon that it will fly straight to that mark. Then he may escape such a

185

devastating verdict as an unsparing listener once visited upon a particular sermon—"like an Indian arrow that has lost its head: all feathers and no point."

Nor is it enough that the man himself should know what he means to say. He must make certain too that the congregation shall know. Concerning this, there is a suggestion as acute as it is original from the "Colonel in the Theological Seminary" of Crothers' essay already referred to in Chapter Three.

I went to church yesterday and witnessed a series of operations that filled me with dismay. The minister began by seizing a text as a base of operations. I observed that the base was not secure, but this made less difference, as he was evidently prepared to change his base if the exigencies of the engagement demanded it. His first mistake was one of overcaution In order to defend himself from an attack from the Higher Critics, he had strengthened his front by barbed wire entanglements in the way of exegesis. This was an error of judgment, as the Higher Critics were not on the field, at least in sufficient force to take the offensive. The entanglements intended to keep a hypothetical foe from getting at him prevented him from getting at once at the real enemy. He thus lost the psychological moment for attack.

While he was endeavoring to extricate himself from his own defenses I trembled for the issue of the affair. Having finally emerged into the open, he was apparently prepared for vigorous operations. I watched intently for the development of his plan. I was bewildered by the rapidity of his evolutions. With a sudden access of courage he would make a wild charge against an ancient line of breastworks which had long been evacuated. Then he would sweep across the whole field of thought, under cover of his artillery, which was evidently not furnished with accurate range-finders. The next minute he would be engaged in a frontal attack on the entrenched position of Modern Science. Just as his forces approached the critical point, he halted and retreated to his textual base. Re-forming his shattered forces, he would sally forth in a new direction.

At first I attributed to him a masterly strategy in so long concealing his true objective. He was, I thought, only reconnoitering in force, before calling up his reserves and delivering a decisive blow at an unexpected point.

At last the suspicion came that he had no objective, and that he didn't even know that he should have one. He had never pondered the text about the futility of fighting as "one that beateth the air."

As we came away a parishioner remarked, "That was a fine effort, this morning."

"An effort at what?" I inquired.[2]

In order that a congregation may surely not be left asking, "An effort at what?" the man who is preparing his sermon may well write down in one short, specific sentence what the essential purpose of the sermon is. For example, when Frederick W. Robertson began to write the great sermon on Elijah which was referred to in Chapter Nine, he might imaginably have set down something like this: "My purpose is to show through the story of Elijah the nature of despondency, and to help every man to understand how despondency like Elijah's may come to him and how God can take it away." Such a sentence may not be put bodily into the sermon, but the formulation of it will be like a compass needle that can control the direction of every paragraph and sentence that the sermon does contain. And this direction of the sermon can be made unswerving to its maximum degree if the preacher will also pin-point it in a title, concise and exact. If there is a printed bulletin of the Sunday services, it can be given there; but in any case the preacher is held the steadier because he has brought it to a focus. Note the suggestive power of

[2] *Op. cit.*, pp. 213-15. Used by permission of Houghton Mifflin Co.

some of the titles of the published sermons of Harry Emerson Fosdick: "The Towering Question: Is Christianity Possible?" "The Christian Interpretation of Life," "The High Uses of Trouble," "On Making Christianity Too Easy," "When Life Goes All to Pieces," "The Power to See It Through." The will to express the purpose and the title of a sermon supremely well is worth hard, concentrated thought and time and trouble.

When the preacher has thus set the compass needle of his purpose exactly, then at least he may be saved from such a verdict as is written under one of the pictures in a book of photographs of New England scenes. On a platform at an out-of-doors town meeting a would-be orator with brandishing arms is launched into an impassioned speech. In the crowd before him are two granite-faced farmers. One asks the other, "What's he talking about?" and the other answers, "He don't say."

If, however, a congregation does know substantially what the preacher is talking about, it is also important that it know at this and that point where he has arrived and where he means to go from there. So the preacher needs, not only at the beginning of his sermon but at the end of every main division and at the beginning of the next one, to give unmistakable guideposts for people's thoughts. That is one of the special values of writing out sermons in full. With the words actually there before him the preacher can make sure that each section and each paragraph has been pointed into such accurate and rightly related words that one leads inevitably to the next. Such careful thinking will save a sermon from those wretched vague connectives such as "and now," "and so," and "one further word," which can make it seem to the congregation no more than a string of loose-jointed notions.

188

Of course, also, if a preacher is to make his message completely clear to his congregation, he must use not only proper dictionary words, but words with which these people are familiar. A young minister who began his work in a rough little town, made up of plain people many of whom were poorly educated, kept his ears open as he went about the streets, into homes, and into shops and stores and railroad station. Before he talked on Sundays, he wanted to know how *they* talked. He made a list of the words and phrases they used in the regular concerns of every day. Then he tried to put his sermons into that vocabulary. It meant that many high-sounding terms that he might previously have thought would be impressive had to be left out, but he had the right idea that a gospel that belongs to life can somehow be expressed within the terms that men and women live by. Like Archbishop Cranmer when he took the medieval service books that were in Latin and changed them into an order of worship in the English tongue, he was determined to put God's truth into language "understanded of the people."

2. If the first question a man who starts to write his sermon asks himself should be, "Is it clear?" the second question to follow immediately upon that should be, "Is it interesting and significant?"

A man may have a fairly clear idea of what he means to say, yet the congregation may be equally clear in their own minds that they do not care whether he says it or not. What the preacher is thinking about may mean something to him and yet mean little or nothing to them. In his brief book *Public Speaking—as Listeners Like It!* [3] Richard C. Borden has indicated in pungent fashion some of the resistances which

[3] New York: Harper & Bros., 1935.

may be present in the minds of any audience. The first is what he calls the "ho, hum" mood. He is writing not particularly for preachers, but his down-to-earth advice is mostly as applicable to them as to anybody else. By the "ho, hum" mood he means the kind of half-somnolent resignation with which people may prepare to accept the remarks of the man who faces them for an after-dinner speech or one of some other kind. It is as though they were thinking, "Now what will he have to say, and how long will he take to say it?" Granted that the preacher in church usually encounters a much more favorable attitude than that. The people have come to church willingly—or at least most of them have. They know and probably like their minister, and in their hearts there may be a real desire that he tell them something that will reach them where they live. But the very routine of a sermon every Sunday may produce a kind of mental lassitude which the preacher has to overcome. As John Oman has put it delightfully, "You must still take up your congregation where most of them are, neither down in the depths nor up in the clouds, but in what you might call a depressed yet dogged hopefulness." [4]

And certainly the preacher must reckon with the second possible resistance which Borden suggests. It is the question that may rise in the minds of the congregation when the preacher's subject seems remote: "Why bring *that* up?" When that question does rise and when it gets no quick and satisfying answer, the preacher has lost his congregation. His imperative business is to make it evident at the outset that what he has to say is both interesting and significant.

That is the reason why the introduction to a sermon must be conceived and fashioned with the liveliest understanding. It should be not only unmistakably clear, but so expressed

[4] *Concerning the Ministry*, p. 146.

190

that each person in the congregation may instinctively feel, "He is preaching to me and about something that *I* see is important."

There was once a preacher—and the "once" may be, rather, a matter of many instances—who at the beginning of his sermon used to remind his congregation of a boy searching for a piece of money in a mud puddle. For a moment or two with a kind of fascination they would watch him grope in the thick waters, but as he never seemed to find anything, and as they began to suspect that what he was looking for was nothing more than a penny anyhow and perhaps not a bright one at that, they sank into a doleful inattention. All preachers may produce the same result if they do not begin more surely.

Nor will it do to begin with some abstruse idea fetched secondhand from a theological textbook. In that case it will seem to the congregation that the preacher has ballooned up into the stratosphere where they cannot get their breath, so they will simply stay behind and begin to think about something else. Neither, on the other hand, can the introduction be so commonplace that the congregation will suspect concerning what is probably to follow, "We have heard all that before." What is needed instead is an approach so direct and plain and yet of such essential dignity of purpose that the congregation will feel that they are being invited into large areas of thought where their spiritual life will find refreshment.

Here, for example, is the way one of Fosdick's sermons began: " 'Handicapped lives'—that subject probably takes us all in. There may be some young, shining Apollo here who never has been aware of limitations, but one suspects not. At least I never yet knew a man who on intimate acquaintance did not turn out to be dealing with handicaps."

Mark the immediacy of interest in that, and its inclusiveness. In three sentences it has been made plain to the congregation that the sermon will deal with a subject of living urgency, and one which gathers up into its reference every single person who is there.

And listen to this introduction to a sermon by George A. Gordon, a contemporary of Phillips Brooks in Boston, as he preached from the words in the second chapter of the Epistle of James, "the devils also believe and tremble": "This fact I have always regarded as highly creditable to the devils. They had sense enough to believe, and they had conscience enough to fear. Our devils are in a worse plight. They neither believe nor tremble. That is vastly to their intellectual and moral discredit."

Probably the congregation would not antecedently have supposed that they would be interested in a text from the second chapter of James, but it is safe to believe that after they had heard Gordon's opening words, nobody would have been left asking, "Why bring that up?"

If the introduction rouses interest, then the opportunity of the whole sermon is to sustain it. That will be first of all dependent upon clearness of structure. It will depend equally upon the preacher's constant awareness of the particular people to whom he is preaching. Father Bull of England has told how it was his practice to go into the empty church in the week before he was to preach, to kneel down where the congregation would be and to think of the kinds of persons who would be looking up to his face on Sunday, and of the kinds of needs which would be stirring in their hearts. And Jowett has said that when he sat down to write a sermon, he would think of some of his people as standing there watching what he wrote; and he would ask himself continually whether his words and sentences would make the truth real to them.

192

A young minister-to-be, about to graduate from a theological seminary and start out upon his work—in the course of a paper on Studdert-Kennedy, that inspired chaplain with the front-line British troops in the First World War, who could draw the interest and emotion of throngs of men and hold them as it were in the hollow of his hand—understood the truth when he wrote:

There are salient features of this man's method which are vital to anyone preaching at this time. There is the constant attention given to the listener. We do not ask ourselves often enough, who is this listener? What is his life like? What is his vocabulary like? What concerns him most? If the vocabulary of our listener is a limited one, then it is senseless to use big words, old words, or long and complicated sentences. It is best that we swallow our pride in newly learned big words and use the language of the streets and the middle-class living rooms to convey the gospel story. Studdert-Kennedy did not hesitate to get on the level of the people he was addressing. Neither should we hesitate. This is not meant to be done in any condescending way. People are sensitive to anything like condescension. It is meant in the knowledge which was Studdert-Kennedy's and should be ours, that Christ died for all. Christ suffers for all men even yet. It follows on this that we should learn the wisdom of using common analogies and homely examples which reflect common experiences with which all listeners can identify themselves. This is not the easy way out. It is the way of suffering. It is hard to make a great theological truth simple. It is our laziness which makes us sound "intellectual" all the time.

How is such a gift for simplicity and identity to be cultivated? First of all it is cultivated by your attitude of mind. If you love common people and sincerely wish to preach to them, half the battle is won. If you love people, you will work and slave to communicate with them. You will be patient and long-suffering and ready to learn from them. You will take the word "sin," ask what it means to the grocer down the street, see how you can bring him to recognize sin in his own life, find the right words for doing this, the right examples, and then you will bring him to Christ by the hand." [5]

But there are two words we are dealing with. The preacher is to be asking himself about his sermon not only, "Is it interesting?" but, "Is it interesting *and* significant?"

Preaching is not a matter of entertaining a congregation. There are sensational preachers who give the impression of being mainly concerned with that. They will use all sorts of theatrical tricks and startling expressions to rouse a crowd response. But the man of true understanding will not be caught in that shallow mistake. He knows that it is not enough for people to go away from a sermon amused or even admiring and excited. The important thing is that the sermon should have been genuinely significant—the setting up of signposts on a heavenly road and an inspiration to walk with new faithfulness on that way.

3. So we come to the third question a preacher should ask about his sermon: "Is it vivid?"

Often a sermon may be clear so far as the general purpose of the preacher is concerned, and may even have an initial interest which makes the congregation disposed to be attentive, yet may result in having the congregation become more and more apathetic. The reason is because the sermon lacks the third quality which it ought to have. It is not vivid. That is to say, it does not sparkle with analogies to life and experience at those points at which the listener is most alive. It has no illustrative quality. It is like a house with no windows in it, and no matter how elaborate a house it may be, that fact does no good if you cannot see out of it and cannot breathe inside

[5] John Booty, at the Virginia Theological Seminary, 1953.

194

it. Some sermons have just that effect upon the people who at first have tried to listen. They have been led through what looked like an interesting door, but they have got into a dark interior. It is not lighted by any freshening suggestions. It does not look out on any contacts with life. It is the kind of sermon in which, with the best will in the world, one nevertheless will intellectually and emotionally go to sleep.

One of the surest ways by which a man can make all his preaching illustrative and vivid is by accustoming himself to talk to children and to learn—sometimes at first painfully —how to hold their interest. Every man has to talk to children on occasions, in Sunday school or elsewhere; and some men whose ministry is richest have established the custom of a three-minute talk to them in the early part of the regular Sunday morning service in church. Nobody can hold the attention of children if he speaks in abstractions. Whatever he tells them must be concrete and graphic. They will not listen to colorless ideas. They must get what he has to say through some clear story that moves swiftly or through a description of some object or event so picturesquely made real to them that they see it—and the point of it—in their imaginations. If a man has made himself responsible for having something to say to the children the next Sunday, he will keep his eyes and ears open all week for suggestions that will spark his mind and give point to his expressions.

That same vividness of thought and speech should go into his preaching to adults. The secret of it is in what Peter Marshall heard a teacher say and never forgot. "Gentlemen, in writing your sermons, I beg of you, use *a sanctified imagination.*" [6] It is a "sanctified imagination" that can lift a sermon up into the realm of poetry. For poetry is not confined

[6] Catherine Marshall, *A Man Called Peter.*

to rhymed syllables; its spirit can be in what has the outward form of prose, but which gives wings to thought by its high and beautiful suggestion. Its quality is that it does not deal with abstractions. "It talks in figures, images and symbols; it does not argue; it does not draw morals; it paints the idea in pictures; it doesn't 'exhaust the subject,' but puts it . . . in a few bold strokes; it lets the truth it expresses make its own appeal; its assumes that the reader [or listener] will also have some imagination, and allows him to use it." [7]

In that sense the parables of Jesus have the infinite lift of poetry. The greatest and most moving preachers have had that quality. It was so with John Donne, with Frederick W. Robertson, with Phillips Brooks. And that quality reappears whenever men perceive truth and embody it not in flat statements but in similes and comparisons which make their listeners *feel* and *see* the glory they transmit.

A notable example from contemporary preaching of the kind of imagination that makes a sermon superlatively vivid is in "The Mountains of God," by Charles W. Gilkey, formerly dean of the chapel of the University of Chicago. Its inspiration came from a remembered day in the Swiss Alps when he gazed at the snowy summit of the Jungfrau, "incredibly beautiful to look upon."

It might have been a summer afternoon cloud, huge and soft and white in the sunlight, but certain soon to dissolve, or it might be the snowy summit of the Jungfrau. Which was it? For the moment, as we sat there, our eyes could not tell.

As we sat watching that mystery in the sky, it suddenly flashed upon me that there before us in symbol was the characteristic question and perplexity of our half-incredulous modern age about

[7] Carl S. Patton, *The Preparation and Delivery of Sermons* (New York: Willett, Clark & Co., 1938), pp. 93-94.

religion. . . . Many . . . feel about it all very much as we felt looking up at the Jungfrau. . . . Religion is certainly very beautiful as it shines there in our human sky, hanging mysteriously between the heaven above us and the earth beneath us, with all the light of our deepest longings and highest aspirations upon it. We should very much like to believe it true. But is it really any more than a summer cloud, born of our traditions and habits and hopes, and reasonably certain to dissolve and disappear when the clear dry light of our modern science and philosophy have worked on it a little longer? Or is it really, as it claims, the summit of all human life and experience, where men may actually meet the Invisible God above them, and become themselves a part of His Eternal Order and Purpose? What is there in religion? [8]

Then upon that magnificent simile of the Jungrau he goes on to consider how we may know the fact of religion, as men know the fact of the Jungfrau, even when it looks incredible or when—as on cloudy days—it cannot be seen at all.

We know the *reality* of religion, as we know the reality of the Jungfrau, (1) because we can check present perplexities by past experience, the days when we cannot see it by the days when we did; (2) because as the Swiss mountaineer knows the constant influence of the mountain, "precipitating the snow and rain that water his garden and provide pasture for his flocks," just so the best evidence of religion is the "stimulating and molding influence which it can and does bring to bear throughout the whole range of higher human living"; [9] and (3) because by courage and discipline a man may climb the mountain heights of experience himself.

We can know the *power* of religion which comes from communion with God in worship and prayer, the results of which

[8] *Best Sermons, 1924*, Joseph Fort Newton, ed. (New York: Harcourt, Brace & Co., 1924), pp. 105-6. Used by permission of the publisher.
[9] *Ibid.*, pp. 112, 113.

are plain to see even when the process is obscure to trace, just as one sees the power of the Jungfrau in the dynamos driven by the "white coal" of the water pouring from the mountain's height and "made up from a thousand trickling rivulets fed by the slow glaciers and the eternal snows." [10]

And finally one can know religion, as one supremely knows the Jungfrau, by *adventure*. The great heights most men do not attain by themselves alone—nor yet without a guide. "So Jesus Christ comes to each one of us, as we catch sight of the heights of life, the presence of God, the world unseen and eternal; and feel in our deepest souls their challenge and claim upon us. His hand rests in comradeship and encouragement upon our shoulder; His outstretched arm points out the climbing path ahead; His voice speaks, quiet but confident, in our ear. 'Come, I've been there. I know the way. Follow me, and we will go together.' " [11]

Such sermons as that on the "Mountains of God" are more rare than they ought to be. Too many men convey the great truths as drably and thinly as though they were making a paper bag to put them in. But the man whose mind is pictorial and who has trained it to become increasingly so by observation and by much reading, particularly in poetry, is like one who lifts a curtain at a window outside of which is the whole fresh wonder of the world at dawn.

Where shall a man find the suggestions that will illuminate his sermons? Everywhere in the whole universe of nature and of human life. From all his reading. From observation of the natural world and the comings and goings of everyday life. From flowers and fields and trees and sky and stars. From city

[10] *Ibid.*, p. 116.
[11] *Ibid.*, p. 122.

and country. From seas and ships and rivers and hills and farmlands and farmers. From men and women in their work and their play, their laughter and their tears. No man who looks upon life with sensitive and sympathetic eyes can fail to find there the innumerable visible suggestions of the invisible realities of God.

A "sanctified imagination" will enable a man to look at human life in a way that enables him to wake in men and women who listen to him those associations and those beautiful overtones of meaning that will make his whole message vivid. Listen, for example, to these words in a sermon of Gaius Glenn Atkins and feel how they come like wakening music. Speaking of an old, familiar hymn, he said:

It has the gift to evoke the sound of voices we no longer hear, the touch of hands that are still. It recalls country churches and summer Sabbath mornings, men and women whose faces were grave and strong and dear; restless children (perhaps we were some of them); through open windows of plain glass the half-heard sound of horses shaking their harness and the gleam of marble or slate headstones beneath which the dead were at the rest they had so laboriously earned.[12]

Vividness in a sermon, which is a pearl of great price, cannot be picked up casually or cheaply bought. To attain it, the man who is to preach must brood with sensitive thought and sympathy upon the quivering realities of life; and he must seek with eager and unwearying thoroughness for the right and living word. The dull or slovenly writer or speaker may be content to state a fact in commonplace, general terms that produce no more of an impression than that of a print made from an underexposed negative, gray and flat and featureless.

[12] Quoted by Patton, op. cit., p. 69.

199

"It was a very enjoyable experience"—but *why* enjoyable? "It was a beautiful view"—but what exactly was in the view, and what was the nature of the beauty? Among the preachers of the mid–twentieth century Peter Marshall was a shining exemplar of that inspired artistry in conception and in words which comes as a gift to some men, but which every man in some measure—and increasingly—can attain. Consider these scattered sentences from his sermons, and note how the words have color and movement that make the listener not only hear about but live within the beauty he evokes:

There is no disgrace in being homesick. At times, I have felt the tugging of those invisible fingers and heard the whispering of those voices. . . . I have longed for the northland. . . . To see again the low stone houses, the swelling hills, the white tails of the waterfalls.

I wanted to hear again the gentle low voices of the women and the music of the gaelic tongue. . . . "Guid save us a' . . ."; to smell the delicate fragrance of bluebells in the spring and the rhododendron; to hear the mavis sing . . . and the lark.

I have wanted to see the long twilights, to look out over the waters of the Firth, and be grateful to God that there was still more of Scotland beyond.

Or feel the instant power of words like these:

It was strangely dark.
A thunderstorm was blowing up from the mountains and the clouds hid the sun. . . .
People looked up at the sky and became frightened. . . .
They stood blinking at flashes of lightning like daggers of fire.[13]

His discouragements had come in a melancholy procession to sit down in dejected rows in the chapel of his heart.

[13] *Mr. Jones, Meet the Master*, pp. 76, 91. Used by permission of Fleming H. Revell Co.

Mountain piled upon mountain like frozen thunder.[14]

Who can listen to such similes as those and not perceive what vividness in language can be?

It is not of course the elaborate word that makes for vividness. Nor is it many words that make for vividness. No one would wisely imitate a certain loquacious Congressman of whom it was said that "he never used one word if two would do as well." It is sometimes a stripped simplicity of style that will carry a thought home like the thrust of a sword. Every period has its own vocabulary which has not grown dull with routine usage but is keen-edged and unmistakable. Any preacher would do well to study the incisiveness with which some of the brilliant journalists write—as in the "Talk of the Town" in the front of any issue of *The New Yorker*. And, above all, the words that count are the vital words— the words that call up pictures of sound and color and movement in the mind. These are the words that poets use, and the man who is to preach should read poetry, and learn to love it, if his own expression is to rise above the dusty ground.

Let every preacher thank God for the magical beauty and power of the language which the long generations have fashioned for us, and reverently seek to be an artist in its use. Let him not be afraid to aim for nobility of speech. Young preachers are sometimes warned against "purple patches" in their sermons, and it is a right warning if what is meant are pieces of pretentious rhetoric sewed on in borrowed scraps. Grandiloquent language can be ridiculous, and secondhand adornments, such as anecdotes and sentimental poems drawn from some wretched book of "sermon aids," can make a sermon sound like the artificial voice of a ventriloquist. But no

[14] *A Man Called Peter.*

"purple patches" will be needed when a sermon is of royal weave all through, and no quotations of artificial eloquence will tempt the man who has attained a natural eloquence of his own. Humbly and reverently every man can aim at that. Let him bravely cultivate whatever gift of imagination, of vivid language, of genuine appeal to people, he may possess. Let him remember that every skill he can learn will magnify his message for God. So, without imitating anyone else, he can lift the range and sweep of his preaching to that spontaneous nobility which belongs to any man who is giving the utmost that his trained and devoted self can win.

4. And now we come to the final point. It is not enough that a sermon should be clear and interesting and vivid. The supreme question remains: Is it convincing?

People will be asking ultimately of any spoken word, as Borden has expressed it, "For instance?" and "So what?" They are not content with generalities. They want to know concretely what the speaker means, and what solid facts there are to illustrate and prove his declarations. And they want to know what all that he has said has come to. What difference does it make? And what is his conclusion?

As to the *conclusion* of a sermon the first necessity for the preacher is that he shall *have* one. Nothing may be more exasperating for a congregation than for a man to say "finally" and then wander on with aimless and stumbling remarks that include a "now to sum up" and "one word more"—until the people are left with no question in their minds except "When will he stop?"

It has been rightly said that more important than the subject of the sermon is the object of the sermon. Everything that is thought and said must move in a straight, sure line toward

202

a climax foreseen by the preacher, and so developed that it will bring enrichment to those who listen. Two thirds of the time and thought of the man who is writing a sermon may well be spent in trying to make as unmistakable and powerful as he can the last one third of it. Failure in this is what makes so many sermons inconsequential. They may have some pleasant vistas along their course, but presently it begins to seem that they are going nowhere. Like a meandering river, the thought of the preacher twists into confused diversions or is slowed down in eddies of irrelevant matters, and at the end peters out into the split streams of a shallow delta with no clear central channel running to the sea.

One chief reason for this is that it is much easier to expatiate on the barriers to conclusive thought than it is to do the hard thinking that will break through them. There was an old clergyman in New Haven, Connecticut, in the 1800's who preached every Sunday morning to a congregation made up in considerable measure of Yale undergraduates, who came to church not because they particularly wanted to, but because by the rule of compulsory chapel or church attendance then existing they had to go somewhere. The old doctor, moved perhaps by the idea that he must be erudite, used to begin nearly every sermon by announcing his text and then saying, "This subject bristles with difficulties." He would then outline the fearsome array of difficulties that the subject might involve, like a navigator speculating on the hidden contact mines that might lie beneath the surface of the channel through which the sermon was supposed to steer. In this preoccupation he would make the difficulties seem worse and worse, until suddenly an ominous sign would warn him that the customary hour for the service to conclude had nearly come. He would then announce, "My watch admonishes me" (though it was not his watch, but the shuffling of the feet of the Yale undergraduates, that admonished him) "that my time is almost up. Did time permit, all these difficulties could be cleared away; but we will now rise and sing the 250th hymn." The result was that every Sunday he presented a new network of difficulties, and nobody ever learned just how to get through to open water on the other side.

But what people want is a positive message. "For instance?" and "So what?" are stubborn demands. None the less actually if not out loud men and women will be saying to the preacher: "What do you mean when you say that we can know the love of God, that we can find help in prayer, that we can have new life in Christ, that we can have all the other experiences you speak about in large assurances? Just when and where and how?" And when they have been told truth which they begin concretely to understand, then the final need is for clear indication of what must follow for thought and will and action.

When a man goes to a physician, he does not want to come away with no other word than, "I see that somehow you don't feel so well and you ought to feel better." He wants to be confident that the doctor knows specifically what is the matter with him, knows how to help him, and is going to tell him with friendly plainness what to do next. When a congregation comes to listen to a preacher who is supposed to be a physician of their souls, they want something equally convincing; and every sermon must measure up as fully as it can to that imperative desire.

The conviction which a sermon should carry cannot be conveyed only in its final words, and certainly not in any climactic burst of rhetorical exhortation. Its convincingness must be the product of the sure and steady message that has been building up from the beginning. But it will be powerfully affected by the skill with which the preacher shapes his conclusion. In form the conclusion should be brief. It should not introduce new ideas, but gather up into swift summary those which have already been developed and put into them all the warmth and urgency which the truth concentrated there can convey. Sometimes the biblical text, as the ultimate answer from God's word to the questions which the sermon has explored, may come at the end of the sermon instead of at the beginning. If at the beginning, it should be the foundation stone on which the whole succeeding sermon is built; but if it is at the end, it is the focus which all the thought leads up to, as to a burning glass where all the gathered rays burst into flame.

SUGGESTIONS FOR SUPPLEMENTARY READING

See the list of books at the end of Chapter Nine.

CHAPTER ELEVEN

Delivering the Sermon

W HEN the sermon in its structure and content is complete, then comes the final and decisive matter of communicating it to the congregation. How shall this best be done?

One way is for the man to preach from his full manuscript laid there before him in the pulpit. Some members of congregations are disposed to think they will not like this. "We want a preacher to speak straight to us, with nothing in between," they say. And their desire may be justified. When a preacher keeps his eyes down as though he were uneasily deciphering the written words, or if he bobs his head up to look at the congregation but does so hastily as though he were continually afraid of losing his place, then something *has* come in between. Instead of a preacher directly and vitally in contact with people, preacher and people are subtly separated by the shuffled sheets of paper. And that paper can be enough to act as insulation and to keep any electric contact from coming through.

Nevertheless some of the greatest messengers of God's truth have preached, and preach now, from a manuscript. This method can have obvious advantages. It enables a man not only to be sure of what he means to say, but to be sure also that he will say it in exactly the proportions of the several

206

points in which he had meant to say it, and that when he has said it, he will stop. It has the further advantage of conveying the precision of phrase and the ordered beauty of rightly chosen words which may not be easy to recapture when the man has to shape his sentences as he goes along. But the crucial requirement in a sermon delivered from a manuscript is that it shall be *preached*, and not merely *read*. This means that the manuscript shall have been gone over so often and so meditatively that the preacher's whole mind and spirit are possessed by it to the point where its message will pour through him alive and new. A soul like Phillips Brooks could so preach from a manuscript that he, and it, and the people together were caught up in one tremendous flame of divine communication.

Another method is for a man to try to memorize verbatim what he has written and thus reproduce the manuscript exactly, not from visible pages, but from an inner vision of what is written on the tablets of his mind. But this *memoriter* preaching is dangerous, both because the congregation may detect an artificial sound as though they were listening to a piece of declamation, and because if memory slips, there may be a blank and disastrous silence.

There is another way toward what may be the most effective mastery. When a man has written his sermon, he may study it deeply and commune with its message until its whole substance and the characteristic manner and rhythm of its expression vibrate again in him, but without any painful effort to get its words by heart. He may make, if he wishes, a digest of the main divisions and subdivisions of his sermon, so specific and so immediately legible that he can see what he wants to at a glance and take that with him into the pulpit. Or he can leave every written word behind and still be con-

207

fident that what he has written will be substantially reproduced in his utterance, but with the added immediacy of those subtle adjustments of speech which are keyed to the response that comes to him from the listening congregation.

As concerning all these forms of delivery, it has been assumed that the sermon has first been written out in full. Nothing that was said as to the importance of this is to be retracted. At the same time it is true, in the words of the great Apostle, that "there are diversities of gifts." There are some men who simply have no flair for writing. They will lament that when they do try to write something out, what they write is stilted and ineffective. It is of course a perilous matter for a man to come lightly to that conclusion concerning himself. He may decide that he cannot write only because he does not want to and is too lazy to try. But if a man in all honesty finds that he cannot write a satisfactory sermon, then let him follow his own method of such structure of notes as he finds most effective; yet let him put into his method no less honesty of devotion and thoroughgoing work than a manuscript preacher puts into his. If he is not to wrestle with words on paper, let him wrestle with ideas in his mind, until he is sure that he sees them there all clearly marshaled for his purpose and ready to come out into his speech with the clean definiteness which can be given only by much discipline of mind and heart.

If one is to preach sermons that will deepen the thought and enrich the spirit of his people, he should be carrying in his mind, for conscious and subconscious meditation, some of the subjects which his experience or his reading have suggested to him, and which he has noted down, perhaps long before. At the beginning of the week he should determine what he will preach upon on the coming Sunday. Early in his ministry he should make a schedule for his sermon preparation and discipline himself to observe it. By Thursday or Friday his sermon should be essentially completed. So he will be delivered from the harried impotence of those who let all sorts of excuses push off the preparation of a sermon to the fag end of the week and leave the mind like a nervous hen scratching in straw for some chance grain. Instead of that the man who is to preach will know that he has something real to give his people, and in the final days or hours before Sunday he can be linking it in his imagination with them and with their needs, and lifting it up in quiet prayer for the blessing of God.

If there are to be two sermons on Sunday, the preacher may not be able to write out both; and his evening sermons may need to be preached from outlines. Also it may happen sometimes that after a man has expected to preach a particular sermon, some crucial incident in his congregation or community, or some deep spiritual experience of his own, may make him sure that he is called—even at almost the last moment—to preach on that. For both these needs his faithful practice of writing out one sermon each week will be his fortification. The ability to concentrate and to put thought into direct expression which that discipline is continually giving him will carry over into those sermons which he cannot write.

The sermon is a great part, but nevertheless only a part, of something larger. It is a grievous perversion if the preacher thinks of what goes before it as merely the "preliminaries." The sermon fits into the whole order of service, and in his selection of hymns, in his prayers, and in the reverent arrangement and conduct of every aspect of worship the minister should be creating for his people a harmonious whole. From the first moment to the last his business is to bring them nearer God, and it is for the culminating expression of this purpose that he goes up the pulpit steps.

Back of him now is all the thorough preparation of the sermon. Back of him also should be the ingrained knowledge of how he is to deliver it. This is not to be a constricting self-consciousness of rules at that moment to be painfully remembered and applied. Rather it is to be the natural expression of what he has already understood and made instinctive.

Begin deliberately. Look at the congregation, and let the response of their attention come back. There is always a moment or two when the people are settling in the pews, straightening this or that, and becoming quiet and undistracted. Do not seem to jerk them into listening. The start of a sermon should be like the start of a train. The conductor gives his signal of "all aboard." The doors are shut. Then the engineer puts the train in motion, not with a sudden blast of steam that would throw people out of their seats, but so that there is a sure but gentle awareness that the train is moving.

Do not begin too high, either in pitch of voice or in rhetorical flight. A voice pitched too high will make the sermon shrill. "Choose," says one who is a minister and has previously been a musician, choirmaster, and an expert trainer of voices, "a moderate pitch, slightly above conversational pitch for a low voice, slightly below for a high voice. Avoid monotony by judicious variations in pitch based upon meaning and feeling." [1] And do not start with some rhetorical rocket.

[1] Lowell P. Beveridge, associate professor of speech and music, Virginia Theological Seminary.

A sermon that starts with high-flown words will then have nowhere to come but down.

Speak slowly enough to be understood, but without halting or stumbling—and without pausing in wrong places and splitting the words in a sentence illogically, as some preachers unconsciously do. Vary speed according to the context, and so avoid the monotony which dulls attention. Allow for spacing, to highlight the structure of the sermon.

Speak distinctly. Poor articulation can be a thorn in the flesh of the preacher—and it may put thorns of irritation into the flesh of the congregation. There is a natural fear of the sort of precision in speech which the preacher may imagine to seem artificial, but there is a trained and disciplined art of clear and finished speech which is the reverse of artificial and which overcomes the sloppiness that is inexcusable.

Good speaking involves the whole body: stance, posture, breathing. Do not clutch the pulpit or lean on it, for to do either can result in hunched shoulders and constricted breathing. Let the whole self be free. Planned and practiced gestures are a theatrical abomination, but in every sermon preached from a man's whole heart there will be a living vigor and vividness that will be instinctively dramatic. No man will stand stock-still and expressionless when he meets a friend on the street and tells him of something exciting that has just happened. How much less should he be stock-still and expressionless in the pulpit. Every part of the man bringing a message of God should be alive: the look in his eyes, the changing expression of his face, the intonation of his voice, and those strong, free movements of arm and hand which give sweep and power to the spoken word.

These principles should belong to the preacher, not in the

211

forefront of his attention, but in his subconscious mind, planted there—it is to be hoped—long before.

For there before him are the faces of the men and women to whom he is to speak. In two aspects their human need will draw his mind and heart. He may think of them as single souls, each with his or her own unique hope and longing and hidden loneliness. "I know what I say to myself," Fosdick has stated, "before anything else when I get into that pulpit. There is in this congregation one person who needs what I am going to say. Oh, God, let me get at him! So I can forget the crowd." [2] Neither he nor any other preacher can know where in the congregation the individual who most needs the sermon's message may be sitting, nor who that person may be. But a message conceived and directed with the passionate eagerness of a personal concern will reach not only one individual but many, and all over the church there will be men and women who will be saying "He has looked into my heart, and he is speaking home to me."

But there is another way of feeling that pull of a congregation. Here beneath the pulpit is not only this individual or that; here is humanity itself; here are the glory and the ignominy, the power and the pathos, of mankind. Some day the preacher will feel the terrible but infinitely inspiring demand of that. The generation born of two world wars is anxious, troubled, and bewildered. No man can preach to it if he has lived in an ivory tower and if his sermons are nothing but indifferent ideas put together in the prim aloofness of ecclesiastical privilege which leaves him blandly ignorant of what ordinary people are up against. His knowl-

[2] Gertrude Samuels, "Fosdick at 75—Still a Rebel," New York *Times* *Magazine*, May 24, 1953, p. 64.

edge must come not only from books in his study, but from the actual life that goes up and down the street. He must have tried to be sensitive to the fears, the apprehensions, and the confused hopes that belong to an actual generation. He will need to be able to say, as the prophet Ezekiel said of the exiles in Babylon, "I came to them . . . , and I sat where they sat" (Ezek. 3:14). For the men and women of a modern generation may be like exiles, separated from their lost religious traditions yet wistful to recover them, depressed but wanting not to become despondent, waiting for a voice that will make them believe in the future and gird themselves to meet it. All this the man in the pulpit can be aware of as he looks out over a congregation and sees its people not as single persons with their separating idiosyncrasies, but as one living part of the destiny of our race. It will not be a matter then of speaking only to particular needs; through them he will be reaching down also to a vaster and more solemn need—the need of all human beings to believe that history is not played out, and that despite all the dark aspects of years that may be tragic there is a greatness in human souls which God's grace can use as the instruments of his victory. That is the message the Christian preacher may be inspired to bring, and no more thrilling moment can be his than the moment when he feels the soul of a whole human group reach up to him to be baptized with a heavenly flame.

SUGGESTIONS FOR SUPPLEMENTARY READING

Broadus, John A. On the Preparation and Delivery of Sermons. New and rev. ed. by J. B. Weatherspoon. New York: Harper & Bros., 1944.

Harper, Ralph M. The Voice Governor. New York: G. Schirmer, Inc., 1945.

Patton, Carl S. *The Preparation and Delivery of Sermons.* New York: Willett, Clark & Co., 1938.

Rogers, Clement F. *The Parson Preaching.* New York: The Macmillan Co., 1949. Ch. 4.

Winans, James A. *Speech Making.* New York: D. Appleton-Century Co., Inc., 1938.

"Finally, Brethren"

THESE WORDS, WHICH stand as a title for the final pages of this book, come, as will be recognized, from the beautiful passage which Paul the apostle wrote as part of the climax of his letter to the Philippians. He was urging them to remember all that they knew and had experienced that was true, honest, just, pure, lovely, and of good report. "If there be any virtue, and if there be any praise," he said—or as the Revised Standard Version has it, "if there is any excellence, if there is anything worthy of praise"—"think on these things."

It is not always easy to follow that counsel. Sometimes the realities round us seem far from excellent. In people and in affairs it may appear that there is much that would be subject to ill report rather than to good report. Not only contemporary literature but also contemporary theology may often accentuate that impression. It is even possible for the whole horizon of thought and expectation to darken, and for men to believe that human history moves on toward a crisis of disaster, until truth seems to echo in the words of the old hymn that comes down from Bernard of Clairvaux:

> The world is very evil;
> The times are waxing late.

215

But nevertheless, and all the more, the Christian preacher must turn his own thoughts, and his people's thoughts, in the direction where Paul bade the Christians of his time to look —toward what is hopeful and heartening. Men and women of the present need that message of reality. The prophet Isaiah promised to those who wait upon the Lord that "they shall mount up with wings as eagles; they shall run, and not be weary; and they shall walk, and not faint." The mounting up on eagles' wings of some triumphant exaltation may not always come, nor is it always possible with quick and glad accomplishment to run. The pace of the spiritual advance for individuals and for society may so slow down that people could become discouraged and begin to believe that life is going nowhere. But the climax of Isaiah's promise is exactly in those words that might appear to be an anticlimax: "They shall walk, and not faint." That is what many men and women are actually doing, and that is what the Christian preacher can help them know that all can do. God be thanked that he does give the rare and glorious moments of winged inspiration and the hours of enthusiastic running, but the great ends of life may depend upon the blessed power to "walk and not faint." It will give a new warmth and joy to all preaching if each man who is to preach remembers the men and women who thus keep going. Let him reflect upon the excellence and the facts worthy of praise in them—in all those who every day are following the ways of the ordinary duty that has no drumbeat; the steady and faithful and dependable people; the man at his honest work and the woman in the home who without any fanfare take up the responsibilities God has given them and will never faint, no matter how long may be the road. Because there *is* virtue and there *is* praise, let him "think on these things."

But the minister who thus sees and encourages the aspects of excellence in his people knows that these are not their own creation. They come from something mightier. They are the reflections of the supreme virtue and the supreme reason for thanksgiving and praise—the power that has been let loose through the crucified and risen Saviour. Over the high altar of Westminster Abbey, above the spot where generation after generation the sovereigns of England have been crowned, are inscribed the words from this great promise of the book of Revelation: "The kingdoms of this world are become the kingdoms of our Lord, and of his Christ; and he shall reign for ever and ever." It is in that faith that the Christian preacher can strengthen men and women to overcome the evil in themselves and to believe even in dark times that they are linked with Him who shall overcome the evil of the world.

It is this gospel then, this good news of hope and courage, that every man in a Christian pulpit is commissioned to preach. Who can ever measure or exhaust the greatness of that opportunity? The young man will know how much there is ahead for him to strive toward; the man of more maturity, if he is reverent and humble, will equally know that too. By all his study and experience, by his growing knowledge of human life and of his own soul and of his Lord, and through his relative successes and his humiliations, his conception of what preaching should become will be glorified and enlarged. And because he knows that he can never rest satisfied with any stage of his accomplishment, he may learn at last to be a not unworthy interpreter of the unsearchable riches of Christ.

Index

219